Here Are the six
other SARK BOOKS:
SUCCULENT WILD WOMAN
Also an AUDIO TAPE
LIVING JUICY
inspiration sandwich
SARK's Journal and PLAY! BOOK
A creATive COMPanion
Also an AUDIOTA
the MAGIC ADDRESS COTTAGE BOOK

the BODACIOUS BOOK of SUCCULENCE

DARING TO LIVE YOUR SUCCULENT WILD LIFE!

BY SARK

A Fireside BOOK

PUBLISHED BY SIMON♥SCHUSTER

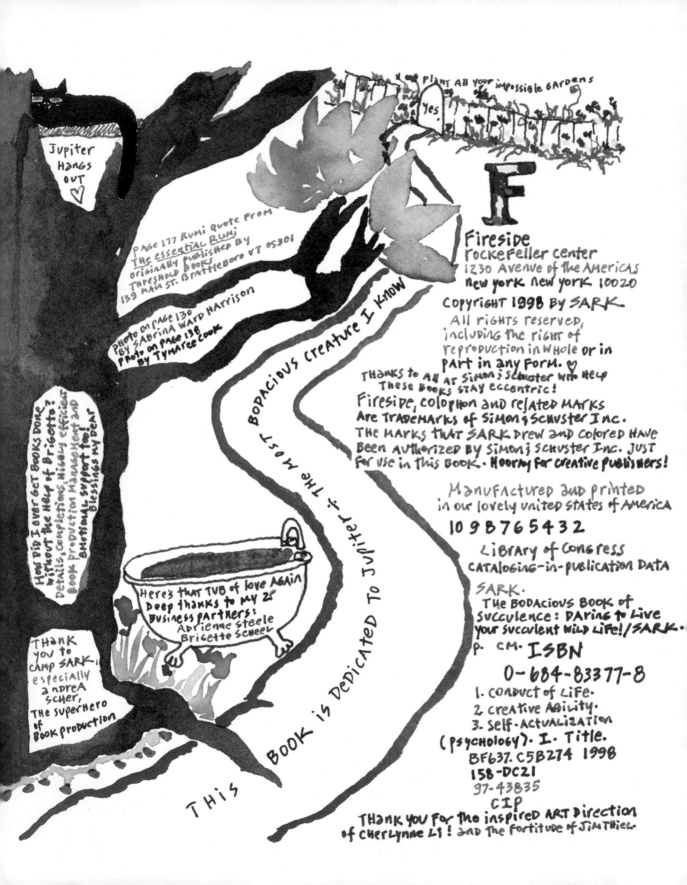

Jupiter HANGS OUT ♡

PLANT ALL your impossible GARDENS

yes.

Page 177 Rumi Quote From The essential RUMI originally published by Threshold books 139 Main St. Brattleboro VT 05301

Photo on page 130 By SABrina Ward Harrison
Photo on page 138 By TyMaree Cook

THE MOST BODACIOUS CREATURE I KNOW

How Did I ever get Books Done without the HeLp of Brigette? Details, Completions, Highly efficient book production Management and emotional support too! Blessings My Dear

Here's that TUB of love Again Deep thanks to my 2 Business partners: Adrienne steele Brigette Scheel

THANK you to CAMP SARK especially ANDREA Scher, THE superhero of Book production

THIS BOOK is DeDicated TO JUpiter

F

Fireside
rockefeller center
1230 Avenue of the Americas
New York New York 10020

THanks to ALL at SiMon; Schuster who HeLp These Books STAY eccentric!

Fireside, colophon and related Marks Are Trademarks of SiMon; Schuster Inc. THE Marks THat SARK Drew and colored have Been Authorized By SiMon; Schuster Inc. JUST For use in this Book. Hooray For creative PublisHers!

Manufactured and printed in our lovely united states of America

10 9 8 7 6 5 4 3 2

Library of Congress CATALOGING-in-publication Data

SARK.
THe BODACIOUS BOOK of Succulence : DAring to Live your Succulent wild Life! / SARK.
p. CM. ISBN
0-684-83377-8
1. CONDUCT of Life.
2. creative Ability.
3. Self-ACTUALIZATION
(psychology). I. Title.
BF637. C5B274 1998
158-DC21
97-43835
CIP

THANK you For the inspired ART Direction of CHerLyNNe Li! and the fortitude of JiM THieL

BODACIOUS:

splendid, BOLD, remarkable

Means: BEING PAID FOR
JUST BEING ALIVE!

Succulence:

is power.Full

Means: WE ARE EACH A GIFT,
EXACTLY AS WE ARE IN
THIS MOMENT, WITH <u>no</u>
improvements!

YOUR SUCCULENT

SHAPES

CHOOSE MORSELS in any order. read RIGHT into A NAP! YOU HAVE NAP permission

Your Bodacious Succulent Life

YOU ARE SUCCULENT even if you don't know it yet. Succulence is A process of Aliveness and Discovery, and it means Living your life in FULL Color, out to the edges, and in celebration of your radiant, eccentric self. BODACIOUS means: SPLENDID, BOLD, and REMARKABLE. THAT'S YOU!

Succulence includes All of you: PARTS THAT MAY Feel lost, trapped, in Hiding, or Broken, As well As your Most FLAMBoyant, extravagant, incandescent PArts. everything in the MiDDLE is succulent too. Our OrDinARy, tender, Jealous, procrastinating, perfectionistic selves.

I wrote the BOOK SUCCULENT WILD WOMAN in 1997 and realized there WAS MUCH More succulence to Write About. I traveled to 35 cities in AMericA and AUSTRALIA and listened to thousands of people tell Me their responses to succulence.

I Found out THAT the First BOOK WAS ABout BeCOMing succulent and thAT THis BOOK is About Actually Living it. I Also realized thAT I wanted to include the Men, AS I SAW

Them at my succulent gatherings, peering over bookshelves, and peeking in around corners. I want to say, "Welcome! We're all succulent together."

Whenever I see tool kits advertised, I always yearn to have a tool for every possible situation (even though I'm too much of a procrastinator to actually fix things). But I do use a mental tool kit, and want to share my succulent pieces with you.

I think our hearts and souls are full of tools, toys, and inventions with which to live our lives. We want brilliant freedom and rich, wide, rare lives. We deserve this.

Sometimes we fall asleep, get lost, or forget that we are such splendid, forgivable, adorable souls. We step into lives that aren't ours, make choices that aren't nourishing, or dance stiffly for years with the wrong partner, or parts of ourselves.

Some say life is short. I say, life is TALL — grab a straw!

I WISH FOR THIS BOOK TO CATAPULT you out of BED and SMACK into the center of one of your DREAMS, or lure you BACK into BED, WHERE you will lie HELPLESSLY LAUGHING AT ALL your PAST Mistakes and Frozen MOMENTS. I WISH For this BOOK to Free the part of your SOUL THAT longs to write epic novels, recite YEATS BY HEART, PLAY A MUSICAL instrument BY MAGIC, or perform in A PLAY ABout your life that you create and Design.

I WISH For this BOOK to Give you A Boost up over the Fence that prevents you From Moving Forward and inWARD.

I Want you to swell up with succulent inspiration and send you FLYING TOWARDS your new creative universe.

A succulent is a plant that gets its nourishment and water from the inside—it replenishes itself.

I wish for you the ability to self-replenish, to be JUICY, ripe, filled to over-FLOWING.

Like the gardens in our hearts

In this book, there are games, surprises, hidden envelopes of money, ultimate rewards and easy tests. You might also find the secrets of the universe, or old band-aids—it depends. It is not a "How-to" book, or even a How-not-to book. It is more of a Being book.   to be yourself

I suggest you Don't Finish it. I suggest you Absorb it by putting it on your head and falling asleep—especially while at work. Like succulent fruit, it can be bitten into at any point. There are no pits. I'm an ordinary woman with a big pen.

11

I HAVE voluminous FAULts — Here is A PARTIAL ALPHABETICAL List: I AM an Angry woman, and HAVe long Been CAlled A Bitch. I AM A Chronic Complainer, and AM Quite Desperate and Deranged. I AM definitely Egotistical, Fearful, Grasping, Hateful, Quite Impatient and A little Bit Insane. Judgmental, But Not A Kleptomaniac. I AM Lost, Maniacal, Not Nice, Overboard, Peevish, Quarrelsome, repressed, Sad, Turbulent, Undecided and Vehement. I AM practicing AT Zen, which is All you can really Do with that!

Later on I will BrAG endlessly and seductively About my GOOD QUALities. THis Book will Hypnotize you into remembering THose Above All others. I AM very GOOD AT this. Do not think you can escape my Brain waves.

I Live in A toolshed I call the MAGic cottage, in San Francisco, with A BLACK CAT and A white Boyfriend. I'M trying to learn to love and Be loveD. So FAr, my CAT is FAr more Advanced AT this than I. You MAY look in AT the process of my Life in this Book and LAUGH.

Please Be KinD if you meet me.

MAKING MORE ALiVE CHOICES

WHEN CONSiDERiNG CHOICES iN YOUR LiFE, THE "MOST ALiVE CHOICE" FEELS LiKE A BiT OF A RiSK, MAKES YOU GiGGLE, OR MAKES THE HAiRS AT THE BACK OF YOUR NECK STAND UP. IT CAN BE A SiMPLE AND TiNY SHiFT, SUCH AS TAKiNG A NEW ROUTE.

THiS NEW ROUTE MiGHT BECKON YOU WiTH COLOR

OR AS LARGE AS MOViNG YOUR WHOLE LiFE SOMEWHERE YOU HAVEN'T LiVED BEFORE.

WE ARE CONSiSTENTLY PRESENTED WiTH CHOiCES. OFTEN, OUR iNNER CRiTiCS RUN THE WHOLE SHOW, AND WE USE A LOT OF LANGUAGE WiTH THESE WORDS:

HAVE TO   SHOULD   I'D BETTER   OR ELSE

THESE CAN BE BULLiES OF THE LANGUAGE WORLD

Sometimes we need to wonder who is making our life choices! We might stumble from one obligation to another, lost in a series of HAVE-TOs.

the HAVE-to CLOCK

Hurry
I'D Better
worry
mistake
No
SHOULD
HAVE to
wrong
worry
Oh Dear

People buy wedding gifts they don't want to buy, attend birthday parties out of guilt or fear, spend time with people they don't even enjoy, or push their children into unwanted activities.   And then we all get crabby!

I remember moving succulently as a young girl in Minnesota, from bike flung to the ground, to deep lawn, to creek bulging with turtles, to eating rhubarb for breakfast and fat, vine-grown tomatoes for lunch.

The most alive choice was a natural step — one to another.

we lived from one gorgeous moment to another.

I think that as adults we become rigidified, encrusted with grudges, wounds, and protective devices that don't work anyway.

person encrusted with grudges

We walk carefully along, checking our purses, pockets, and car keys.

Gone are our BAMBOO WALKING sticks and FLAGS for countries that we've MADE up. I think those things are only gone because we've stopped calling them.

wonder land

We've stopped counting fireflies at DUSK, standing naked in the rain, fingerpainting with our

Feet AND STUFFING A BAG full of costumes and MAKING our "poet's corner" in the BACKYARD, with lanterns and tents MADE out of chenille bedspreads.

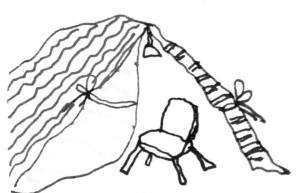

one crooked chair was all we needed

We deserve to be the caretakers for our spirits and dreams, and this means truly sensing and listening for our most alive route. It may not be a common path, or a popular one, yet it will be clearly ours.

"My life is full of mistakes. They're like pebbles that make a good road."

Beatrice Wood

I remember fishing as a young girl and catching a snake — it whipped out of the water, whistling through the reeds and landing in a hissing circle at my feet.

By then it had gotten unhooked, and streaked back into the water. I stood panting and laughing. I felt terrified and alive.

When we can trust what life brings us, I think we can stand in the center of our aliveness

the hissing circle

and meet flying snakes along with the whole wild mystery we call life.

16

Here Are some Alive Choices that May inspire you to Choose your Own:

Paint your Car!...My Car (Venus)

suffered a big gouge in the front bumper from someone's trailer hitch. The repair estimate was $900. Instead of spending that, I donated money to a place called Home Away From Homelessness—a Beach House for homeless Kids.

> eventually, I'd Like my car to Be Covered with A collage of stories of Helping others

Plant Flowers For your Friend...

especially if they Don't seem to Be planting their own!

I CAME HOME FROM A trip to Find that My Friend Brigette HAD Planted Pots And Pots of Brightly Colored Flowers in All My empty Pots!

Donate copies of your FAVorite children's Books to the School or library nearest you...

Books shown: Gone Away Lake · Harold and the Purple Crayon · Pippi Longstocking · Mr. Bass and the Mushroom Planet

Some of My FAVorites

Put up a hanging bar in your house... or place to be easily ¡umop ǝpᴉsdn

Being upside Down Gives us A new perspective

MAKE YOUR OWN BOOK of WHAT YOU'RE GLAD ABOUT:

Here Are SOME PAGES FROM mine

MEDITATING MORE often

EATING DELICIOUS SALADS I've MADE AT HOME

MY WOODEN WIND CHIMES

BEING KINDER to MYSELF

WHAT ARE YOU GLAD ABOUT?

18

Succulent Moves

As we choose to add more succulence to our lives, we will naturally and eagerly be seeking more succulent stories. They will spill out and over!

Here are some of my favorite responses from people who were asked, "What one (small thing) are you willing to do now that will help your life be more succulent?"

"I'm a procrastinator, so I had never filled out my children's baby books. After 46 years, I filled them out with what I could remember and mailed them to each of the kids!"

"To sew my torn long silk kimono and then prance around in it!"

"To stare lovingly into my husband's eyes for 60 seconds."

"I'm going to make a darkroom out of my broom closet."

"instead of trying to have an ORGASM, I'm going to learn how to Be an orgasm."

"The next time my son sings repetitive and annoying songs loudly in the car, I'm going to take a a deep breath, and say, More! More!"

"I'm going to Buy myself sexy new Bras."

"To stand or run naked in the next rain."

"I'm going to wear my colorful scarves... again."

"I'm going to admire and inhale the fragrances of the herb garden I planted. I've never stopped long enough to just do that."

"I'm going to paint with my 2 1/2-year-old daughter. For almost a year she's been saying, 'painting now Mommy?' and before I can answer, she says, 'I know, in a minute?'"

"I'm going to spend one day just being of service to others."

"I'm going to go to Madrid and drive in a red convertible."

You can color around & inside these circles

20

WHAT Are Your succulent Moves?

21

Your Succulent MAP

Begin Here.
As you scan through your life, what areas could use more succulence, more juice?

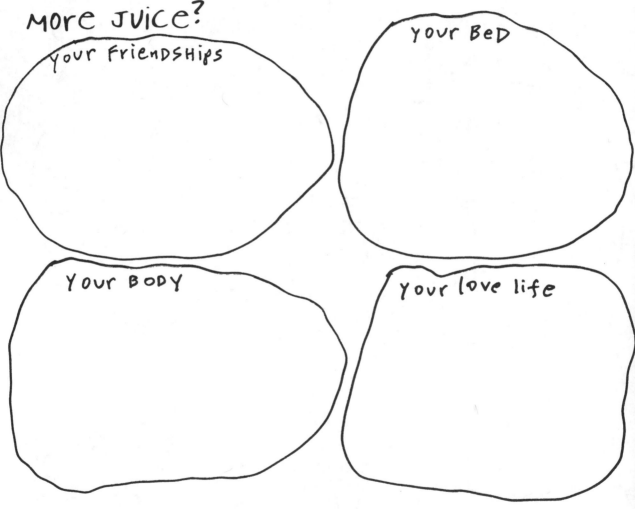

Your Friendships

Your Bed

Your Body

Your love life

Begin to Fill these BUBBLES with succulent scribblings or drawings. Draw out your succulence. . .

YOUR SEXUALITY

YOUR RELATIONSHIP
WITH NATURE

YOUR TIME WITH
CHILDREN

YOUR ADVENTURE LIFE

YOUR TIME WITH
OLD PEOPLE

YOUR SPIRITUALITY

23

Leaps of Faith

Our lives are filled with places where we choose to leap or stay put. One is not better than the other, yet leaping has its advantages.

Let's look at some examples of "leaps of faith." These are points where it is tempting to stay put because it seems "safer."

Ken—who stayed on the graveyard shift in radio as a traffic reporter so he could spend most of every day with his 3-year-old daughter.

Adrienne—who quit a high-paying job as a cosmetic executive, while pregnant, and went on a planned vacation to the Bahamas, trusting that she would create a job she loved by being herself.

Craig—who left a much sought-after position at Disney to follow his dreams.

Christine—who quit her lucrative position in retail to spend time with her

Leaps of faith are well rewarded

FAMily AnD CHOOSE A MOre MEANinGFUl JOB.
rAy- WHO left tHE APPArel inDuStry
AnD New York City to Move
to A COttAGE By tHE SEA in
CArMel AnD live HiS DreAMS.
My GreAt-GrAnDMOtHer PACKED HerSelF
AnD 9 KiDS into tHE CArGO HolD OF A SHiP
AnD SAileD to SOutH AFriCA FroM EnGlAnD,
in SEArCH OF A DiAMOnD Mine. tHE Mine
turneD out to BE A FAlSE ClAiM, SO tHEy
HOMESteADED AnD My GrAnDMOtHer rAn tHE
POSt OFFiCE AnD GenerAl Store.
    My GrAnDMOtHer tHEn tOOK A leAP OF
FAitH AnD MOveD to CAliFOrniA WitH My
GrAnDFAtHer in SEArCH OF A GOlD Mine!
WHiCH AlSO turneD out to BE FAlSE.
    LEAPS OF FAitH Are AlSO tAKen By
StAyinG. IF yOu Are rAiSinG CHilDren
COnSCiOuSly, Or SCHOOlinG tHEM DiFFerently,
yOu Are DEMOnStrAtinG DAily leAPS OF
FAitH.
    COMMitMentS OF All KinDS require leAPS
OF FAitH.

    WHere HAVE yOu Been leAPinG lAtely?

We Are each Directly or indirectly Asked to Fulfill our DreAms And Destiny. Sometimes we crAwl there, or Find ourselves stuck outside of our DreAms.

Leaps of FAith cAn put us in A new spot we couldn't see From where we stood Before.

I think when we hAve the courAge to sepArAte From A non-nourishing love relAtionship, it is A leap of FAith. we mAy feel certAin thAt we will never love AgAin.

A new spot

Sometimes it is A long time Before love surFAces AgAin. it is then thAt we must tAke Another

love surfAces

leAp of FAith within ourselves And trust thAt we Are guiDeD And leD in some wAy.   Trust.

I find myself doing my least leaping with spirituality and love relationships. I do kind of a sock hop of little faith, testing, checking and rechecking for the false bottom, the hidden trap door, the final entrapment. I am constantly (or it feels constant) searching for the exit, the way out, the safe route.

LEAPS OF FAITH

WHERE DO YOU DO YOUR LEAST LEAPING?

MOST?

WHAT DOES FAITH MEAN TO YOU?

WHAT EXAMPLES OF LEAPS OF FAITH ARE IN YOUR HISTORY?

Are there places you would like to leap, but don't know how? leap first in your own heart.

inspiration by phone

Three years ago, I started something called "the inspiration line." It's 3-5 minutes of inspiration recorded by me, monthly. Thousands of people from all over the world call to just listen, or leave me a message.

The messages I make are from my heart and spirit. They include: quotes from poets and writers, moments in nature, admissions of failure and crabbiness, lessons learned, truths sought, and things I "send" tele-phonically to the caller with the help of my guided imagery and their imagination. *people leave the most amazing messages*

The inspiration is very reciprocal, since I listen to the messages and receive back what I put out there.

It's also a rather revolutionary way to be in touch with the readers of my work. I wish it for every author...

415 546 3742 (epic)

wonders of the phone

who enjoys the phone!

This phone line consistently presents the miracles of our collective unconscious and how connected we all are.   it is so full of serendipity!

One woman said, "I call to get the love. Sometimes they are the kindest words I hear all day."

The messages contain my love, which I will continually share, even though I don't "know" the callers. Aren't we funny to wait to show love until we "know" another—as if we ever can?

The messages I receive are almost all warm, funny, or positive—I especially appreciate people's sadnesses or tears—these are gifts of the soul, and certainly inspirational. inspiration is not only positive.

we are all so indelibly connected

How to make your own "inspiration line"

IF you Are DrAwn to this, Choose A nAme tHAt CAn Be your mission For the line: success-possibilities-love-grAtitudes.

You CAn rent A voiceMAil Box For ABout $8 A montH. or use A Home MACHine (GOOD to HAve A sepArAte line, tHouGH).

Decide if you wAnt to cHAnge it rAnDOMly or At A certAin time.

Write out A sAMple messAGe AnD record it to HeAr HOW you sounD.

Smile As you speAk-tHe wArMtH will Be in your worDs. we All wAnt to HeAr More
Be sure to lAuGH!   LAuGHTer

Decide HOW to spreAD the worD ABout your line: newsletter, Fliers, tiny notes on Bulletin BOArDs, AnD of course, worD oF moutH.

resources:
Louise HAY Line 760.431.3600 } exAmples of inspiring lines
Success Hotline   201.743.4690 } cAll And listen!
eFLs voiceMAil   800.348.0500
(to orDer A voiceMAil nvmBer)

Making it Real

Our creative dreams so often stay in our heads, inside drawers, or in journals that we stop opening.

The Hidden Journals

We forget the power of a real thing. When you give a creative dream form, shape, color, or design, it can travel without you to new lands. It then has its own life and is able to speak for itself.

When I wrote my first book, <u>A Creative Companion</u>, I wasn't even sure it was a book. It didn't look very much like other books I had seen, and I was aware of a certain revolutionary quality between its pages. I was just relieved that a thing had been made real, and I could stop trying to describe my vision.

A Creative Companion by SARK

I used a lot of energy for years trying to describe my creative dreams. It is a very tempting thing to do for a creative procrastinator.

Describing the creative dream takes it one step further, but not so much further that you risk being judged, found lacking, or even disliking it yourself!

That type of talking also uses up a precious energy: your creativity. If you explain your creative idea to every new person, you are usually not working with the thing itself—it is not becoming real or visible, and you can be drained by trying to explain it.

In effect, you are not letting your creative dream have wings. and they need wings!

BEAUTIFULL WINGS YOUR DREAM

Once I made my first book real, I could begin another book! "Making it real" also gives dimension and explanation in a way that words don't.

If you say "picture a wonderful tree" to 100 people, you'll probably get that many versions of trees in people's minds.

(We need to see your tree.) The one you've dreamed about, sketched on the backs of paper bags, the one you took photos of in all different seasons.

Your particular vision is very much needed. Making it real is a way for us to experience you without meeting you. Your creative dream can have so many more branches if it exists outside your head.

Making it real also means that it may change shape and color as you work with it. As you create it, new possibilities will leap in, asking to be seen and considered.

There are so many branches outside your head

Your "tree" could turn into a bent old woman, or lovers entwined in the roots.

or a child could crawl out of a tree root!

A POEM COULD LEAP OUT in A DREAM
DURING THE MAKING-it-REAL PROCESS.
 YOU MIGHT MAKE it REAL
AND HATE THE RESULT. WORK
WITH THAT HATE AND MAKE THE
next THING REAL.   SOME OF THE BEST POEMS LEAP OUT

   "All WORTHWHILE ART HAS SOME GOOD
HATRED MIXED into it."

                   ANDREW KENNEDY
   WE ARE NOT in CHARGE OF WHAT
COMES FROM THIS PROCESS. THE REAL
THING MAY CHANGE US. HOW CAN WE
KNOW?

   (RISK it All.)

   YOUR REAL VISION is IMMEASURABLY
VALUABLE AND I DARE YOU TO LET it
OUT.

   LET US All SEE WHAT YOU HAVE
MADE REAL FROM YOUR DREAMS AND
IMAGINATION.

   WE ARE WAITING TO SEE.
WHAT IS inside OF YOU RIGHT NOW THAT YOU CAN
        BEGIN TO MAKE REAL?

MicroMovements
Tiny little BABy steps

MicroMovements Are tiny, tiny little steps you cAn tAke towArds completions in your life.

I'm A recovering ProcrAstinAtor, And I HAve A sHort Attention spAn, so I invented MicroMovements As A method of completing Projects in time spAns of 5 minutes or less. I AlwAys feel like I cAn HAndle Almost Anything for 5 minutes!

clock of Forgiveness

no problem
it's o.k.
eAt
nAp
sleep
Yes
quit
it's o.k.
Go BACK To sleep
cAll lAter

Here's An exAmple of A Project tHAt cAn sit on A list for montHs or even yeArs.

clean THe closet

it's too BiG! noBoDy wAnts To Do it.

ProcrAstinAtors Are greAt mentAl reHeArsers. THey cAn cleAn the closet in their minD Dozens of times witHout Any ActuAl movement!

AnD THen, THere can Be no FAilure! or success...

Here's An example of A
Micromovement:

THursDAY, 10 AM,
open the Door to the closeT.

open

After completing this Micromovement,
you simply choose Another Gentle,
small step.

FriDAY, 2 pM,
TAKe 5 pairs of SHoes off
the shelf and look AT THeM.

WHo BoughT THese SHoes?

It is importAnt to use DAtes And
times As A GuiDance system. It is
eQually importAnt not to tyrAnnize
yourself with the chosen time. if
the time comes, And you simply
cAnnot MAKe A Move, Gently Assign
yourself Another DAte And time.

Gentle
Time

Writing it Down Gets it
out of your HeAD WHere it
can Be sepArAte From you.

All of my 7 published books,
posters, cards, and company exist
due to many thousands and
thousands of micromovements all
strung together. I think of the
micromovements as tiny colored
beads that have helped me be
someone who lives in her dreams
instead of only talking about them.

A string of micromovements

Procrastinators are also great
at beginnings and not as skilled at
completions. I have learned about
the satisfaction of completion. It
is like a circle instead of a line.

started writing children's book — writing — writing — stopped

started children's book writing found artist found publisher editing writing completed chapter

it all stays together in the circle

Most of us have such great dreams
and intentions!
We deserve to complete our creative
dreams and make room for more!

Micromovement Reminders

1. Choose a [tiny] step—something you already know how to do. If you want to write more letters, a good micromovement would be: Tue. 2pm, put stamps and paper and pen in same spot.

2. Write down your micromovement with a date and time. You can always reassign it. It has more value in the material world when it is written down.

   > Tue 2pm
   > put stamps
   > and paper

3. As soon as you've completed your micromovement, choose the next one and write that down.

4. Micromovements resist repetition. Example: "My micromovement is to write in my journal every day for 5 minutes."
   Sound reasonable?

   > We want to / write more in our journals

   It may sound reasonable, but it isn't. Here's why:

The first time we get a headache, or don't feel like writing, or just don't do it, the inner critic lurches forward with pleasure and says, "AHA! see! you can't even write every day for five minutes. You'll never be a writer... BIAH BIAH BIAH."

Simply make it smaller:

> Tomorrow at 8 pm write in my journal for 5 minutes

5. Get micromovement support. Find a friend who is eager to work with micromovements and check in with each other on completion schedules.

   note: Do not engage in fault-finding or sarcasm when you falter. Choose a sensitive and kind friend doing inner critic work.

6. Collect notes about your micromovements all the way through a project, and study how you did it. We often forget our own ways and methods.

7. Be willing to practice this system and continually forget about it, fail at it, yet still have faith in yourself and your creative dreams.

8. Be willing to get smaller. <u>Most micromovements are too large</u>. In fact, we assign ourselves projects that are much too big and then get discouraged by our own inactivity.

More micromovement examples:

I wish to: MAKE A BIG PURPLE PILLOW

Micromovements:

read: lie down.
The purple pillow of dreams

1. Call Nancy Wed 10 AM, ask where she got the great purple fabric
2. Thu 11 AM, put fabric near sewing machine
3. Fri 4 PM, draw 2 types of pillow ideas
4. Sat 2 PM, assemble supplies for 5 minutes
5. Sun 5 PM, sew a tiny purple pillow cover

Continue micromovements until completion.

WISH: To take singing lessons
WISH: To be more creative with the kids
WISH: To write a children's book
WISH: To publish my poetry

Invent or imagine micromovements for each of these wishes.

THe VAlue of your creAtivity

Your creAtivity is An immense force thAt is inside every cell of you. THe vAlue of thAt is immeASurABle. Your creAtivity in Action is so needed By our world And the people in it.

No other person HAs your eccentric Blend of iDeAs, Attitudes, And perceptions.

We cannoT see with (your) eyes!

No MAtter How lumpy or FADED or Boring you feel, your creAtivity is of vAlue. ‿‿ There Are treAsures inside the lumps

Your creAtive thinking cAn sAve lives And souls And feed stArving Artists.

THe CHilDren neeD your creAtivity

You CAnnot sAy, "I'M not very creAtive" until you HAve explored your soul And HeArt's Gifts.

   We Are eACH Born (SO) creAtive—Then we forGet our purpose, or Mission. We Believe our DouBts And FeArs, And slowly stop "BeinG creAtive," As tHouGH it were A sepArAte thinG.

WAKE UP!

THe LiGHT OF
your purpose
Glows BriGHTLy

   step BACK into the liGHt of your creAtive purpose even if you're not sure wHAt it is. WHen people Ask wHAt you Do, reply,

   "I'M A creAtive spirit— I JUST CAMe Here To Help."

Move Freely into your VAluABle creAtivity!

   "WHen AnytHinG Gets FreeD, A zest Goes round the world."
                  Hortense CAlisHer

Doing it anyway

Creativity is there all the time. We're the ones who leave it. We wait for the inspiration to start, yet it's really the other way around—first the action, then the inspiration.

I'm almost never "in the mood" to create something. It never seems to be the right nuance of emotion, or amount of time, or apathy drifts in and whispers things like "why bother," "it won't look the way you want it to anyway," or just "Why?"

Doing it anyway is just that. Create alongside moods. Create when your laundry seems like the most exciting thing in your life.

excited laundry
Going out to
Be Washed
Laundry Doesn't Get out Alone
At very many other times

Create when sickness overtakes you and you can barely walk to the kitchen. Create when you are ecstatically happy. Especially then.

every single BOOK I've written GOeS
tHrouGH terriBle PeriODs OF stuckness.
I WAKe UP FrOM A nAP At MY
"APPOInteD time" to Write, AnD FinD
Myself in sOMe kinD OF eMOtiOnAl BOG,
Or sCAry DreAM resiDue tHAt Feels
like tHe exAct OPPOsite OF CreAtivity.
    We MUst CreAte FrOM tHOse PlACes
tOO. OH, tHe FAntAsy is tHAt We
AWAken in sOMe BeAUtiFUl setting,
exerCise, eAt sOMetHing liGHt AnD
nOUrisHing, sOMeOne kisses Us, tHe
BirDs Begin to twitter, AnD We settle
HAPPily intO OUr CreAtive rOUtine AnD
WOrk HAPPily FOr HOUrs At A time.
    SO MUcH OF liFe is tHe MUnDAne, tHe
AnnOying, tHe Unsettling Or COnFUsing.
OUr PersOnAlity selves Are BUsy
JUDGinG, reHeArsinG, COMPlAininG, Or
PrOteCtinG.

turn off the neGAtive

OH WHy
Bother?
it WOn't
Be tHAt
GOOD
AnyWAy.

(We MUst DO it AnyWAy.) THe AnyWAy
Will leAD Us intO riCHness— tHe
riCHness OF OUr ACtUAl experience, AnD
tHe GiFts OF OUr OWn reAl CreAtivity.

THe BirDs BeGAn TO Twitter...

44

Gifts of Procrastination

There are exquisite pains and gifts within procrastination. The gifts keep us involved

When we put off beginning or completing a creative dream, we escape judgment and failure.

When we procrastinate, we are often mentally or psychically rehearsing our steps and movements.

The steps sometimes lead to the waiting room....

Paralysis lies in wait for procrastinators. Sometimes we lie still in a room, discouraged beyond measure at our own lack of movement.

The waiting room

Procrastination buys us an odd limbo—we are not out of, or into, the thing we dream of. It is the waiting room inside of us.

The inner critics love our procrastination. They can plant all the darkest messages of judgment and failure, and delay us.

Patches of thorns are common

Still, if you procrastinate enough, there will be consequences that may jostle you into a different way of being. THIS JOSTLING CAN SOMETIMES FEEL ALARMING

Also, it is possible to get truly sick and tired of procrastinating, which can cause sudden, gigantic movement, or tiny inroads of activity.

The inertia can actually be the fuel we need to

START TAKE SOME KIND, ANY KIND, TINY inroADs can leAD us TO GiGAntic MoveMents of action or remain present and still with ourselves.

Procrastination is all around us. Whenever I ask a group of people if they consider themselves pro-crastinators, about 80% will raise their hands.

Yet we all think we're the only ones

I consider myself a recovering procrastinator. I'm still discovering and uncovering new things about it. It used to run my life a lot more—

then I began studying it as an actual subject, and trying new approaches to it.

NEW APPROACH

I now have more experience with completion than I ever dreamed possible.

Procrastination can be a mask we wear to avoid being as great as we truly are.

The fear of succeeding is actually more scary than failing.

THE MASK OF PROCRASTINATION

WHO'S really inside?

I invite you to study and reflect upon procrastination in your life. I suggest you learn to use procrastination for its gifts and not just its detriments.

The procrastination of those in our lives also affects us. I invented an acronym for it: P.A.M.L - Procrastination Affecting My Life. You can use this to help note when you are being adversely touched by someone else's procrastination.

Most of us are involved in procrastination to some degree—let's bring it out in the open, speak of it with gentleness and humor—admit when it's crushing us or stopping our joy.

Another active ingredient of procrastination is secrecy. It thrives in our hidden brains. Begin to shine light on it—loosen its grip.

exploring procrastination

Are you aware of procrastination in your life?

How does it affect you?

In what ways do you stop yourself from experiencing joy or success?

When do you first remember feeling procrastination?

Were your parents procrastinators?

is someone close to you a procrastinator?

What gifts do you receive from procrastinating? Pains?

read:

Procrastination   Jane Burka, Ph.D.;
                    Lenora Yven, Ph.D

The Tomorrow
    Trap   Karen E. Peterson, Ph.D

48

WHEN Writing

People often ask, "What is your routine? Do you write at a particular time of the day or night?" I laugh. I'm tempted to make up a story that will sound sensible or inspired, or somehow magnificently creative.

I want to invent an entire routine that will satisfy the questioner.

More often, it is random and ordinary and lucky. It is a balancing act of blood sugar and fear and reckless patterns of avoidance.

The inner critic puffs up and becomes enormous. He stands at the gates, shouting about content, form, and grammar.

His only job is to prevent me from actually writing.

My friend Sabrina asked me, "How do you start? How do you get past the critic?" (run!)

I heard myself reply, "You do anything. You lie, slide on your stomach under the gate, papers in your mouth, you present false papers--whatever gets you past the critic. It doesn't matter. Once you are writing you cannot be stopped."

once you are writing you cannot be stopped

Then, when you have written, you can wave your pages at this critic in vengeful joy. The critic only has one job, and now he can't do it.

The critic is not stronger than you

Sometimes I am astonished that I can write at all. It feels like a flea circus,

MADE OF INTRICATE AND TINY
MOVEMENTS THAT ARE UNSEEN FROM
AFAR, BUT ACTUALLY BUSY MOVING AND
BUILDING.   IT IS HARD TO TRUST THESE UNSEEN MOVEMENTS

   I HAVE LEARNED MORE ABOUT
HONORING THE EMPTY TIMES OF NOT
WRITING. MY FRIEND MIRIAM SAID ONE
TIME, "NOTHING IS COMING. ALL I CAN
DO IS BREATHE AND WAIT."

   I CREATE AN ORB FOR THE WRITING
TO BE BORN INTO. THERE ARE RITUALS
FOR THIS: SYSTEMATIC CLEANING AND
ORGANIZING, THE PLAYING OF CERTAIN
MUSIC, AND THE GATHERING OF SILENCE.

THE GATHERING OF SILENCE IS
LIKE CLOUD WATCHING

A CEREMONIAL NAP, OR SEVERAL, THE
INGESTION OF MINDLESS MAGAZINES,
AND THE BALLAST OF ONE GOOD DEEP
NOVEL-READ SLOWLY AND WITH GREAT
PENETRATION.

EARTHLY PARADISE
BY COLETTE

I AM SUBJECT TO SUDDEN FEVERS
AND IMMENSE DREAMS DURING THESE
TIMES. THEY JOLT ME OUT OF BED AND
SLEEP AND SEND ME WANDERING AT
NIGHT.

I FIND I MUST SMELL
THE NIGHT JASMINE AND SOAK
IN MOONLIGHT.

THE NIGHT JASMINE HANGS DOWN
IN FRAGRANT CLUMPS

I CANNOT "CHAT" AND "BANTER"
WITH BREEZY CONVERSATIONS. I
EXPERIENCE MY INTROVERSION MORE
STRONGLY AND FIND IT MORE NECESSARY.

THE
SHAPES
ARE
CURIOUS
AND
DETERMINED

THERE ARE SHAPES
BULGING OUT OF ME. I
CAN FEEL THEM MOVING
INSIDE MY CLOTHES.

I HIDE MY PHONE IN THE
CLOSET. TO SEE IT OR HAVE IT NEAR
ME REMINDS ME OF PEOPLE AND THEIR
GRAVITY, AND OF MY SOCIAL NEEDS.

"WRITING IS LIKE DRIVING AT NIGHT.
YOU CANNOT SEE BEYOND YOUR HEADLIGHTS...
BUT YOU CAN MAKE THE WHOLE TRIP THAT WAY!"
E. L. DOCTOROW

These times of retreat also contain demons for me—loneliness, fear of craziness, obsessive fears, and compulsive actions. Sometimes it feels like writing is the only thing that saves me.

People ask, "How can I be a writer?" I think it is more interesting to explore what happens if you are not a writer. Who do you become without that expression?

The hardest part is starting.

The Pages Are Waiting

HOW TO START

1. Use tricks, games, ploys, bribes, gifts, deceptions, and inventions.

2. Read these authors:

   Natalie Goldberg, Anaïs Nin, Tillie Olsen, Anne Lamott, Julia Cameron, Annie Dillard, Robertson Davies, Henry Miller, Maya Angelou, whoever inspires you.

3. Fill yourself up with inspiration, quotes, comic books, walks in the woods at dawn.

4. Sit in front of blank paper or an empty computer screen for 5 minutes without writing.

5. For 5 minutes, allow yourself to write something. Anything. *scribbles are good*

6. Scribble something.

7. Complete these sentences:
    I cannot write about _____,
    because it might be _____ or,
    _____, or _____.

8. Play "Exhaust the Critic." Here's how: Write the headline "Why I Can't Write" at the top of a piece of paper. Fill this sheet and as many as you need with every tiny, microscopic, annoying, or large reason you can't write. (I commonly fill 4-6 pages when doing this.) Put these pages aside when you can't think of another thing.

WHY

I can't

9. Weave together all the parts of yourself—the young, wise, incompetent, solid, sure—and then close your eyes and jump in—be willing to accept massive imperfections.

Write

10. Play "nourish the writer." Here's how:
Write at the top of a piece of
paper "Why I can write" and go
through your list of why you can't,
and reply positively to every point.
Here are examples from my lists:

I can't write because:	I can write because:
1. I'm fat	1. Write about feeling fat
2. it will be boring	2. Write about boredom
3. no one will read it	3. Write about fear of not being read
4. I need to do laundry	4. Provide space and time for writing
5. people interrupt me	5. Allow time for people too
6. I'm afraid it won't be good	6. your writing usually brings out something good
7. I'm not good enough	7. you are enough you have enough you do enough

Mostly, it empties these thoughts
from your mind and provides space for
new words to be born.

11. Play Parcheesi, Monopoly,
Backgammon, Scrabble, or Bridge.
Here's why: Games provide a
respite from the particular intellectual
parts of the mind used for writing. You
can still ruminate and ponder, and
interact with another person or people.
(Parcheesi is my favorite)

Being Published

I wrote my first book at age 10 (Mice From Mars) and then it took 28 years for me to publish my first "real book," A Creative Companion, at age 38. "One should always be a little improbable." Oscar Wilde

Every publishing story is as unique as the author, and by sharing mine here, perhaps I can inspire you about your own publishing story.

Being published was a dream of mine from the time I got my first library card in 1st grade and started reading a book every day.

Visions of Books Danced in My Head

Books saved my emotional life during years of sibling incest and gave me hope to keep on living.

I eagerly read everything written about being published, and stuffed myself full of biographies of writers and how they lived. Wisdom of the Heart

I dutifully read <u>Writer's</u> <u>Market</u>, and sent out query letters and self-addressed stamped envelopes. I wrote to authors I admire and asked for advice. I yellow-highlighted my favorite publishers in source books and kept track of books they published.

I would order new bank checks just so something of mine was being published! To me, the most marvelous number in the world was the ISBN number on books.

Susan Ariel Rainbow Kennedy aka SARK

My cartoons and art were published in the newspaper for about 6 years, but it wasn't the same as a book.

In 1990, I was contacted by one of the publishers I had admired, who asked to publish my "How to Be an Artist" poster.

I began talking about the books I wanted to write (as I had been talking for at least a decade) and was asked once again, "Why don't you write them?"

How To Be an Artist
Stay loose. learn to watch snails. plant impossible gardens. invite someone dangerous to tea. make little signs that say yes and post them all over your house and there's more...

57

I PrActicAlly PUSHED THE EDITOr OUT
OF THE GATE OF MY GARDEN SO I COULD
try AND Write THE BOOK I'D DrEAMED
ABOUT FOr SO long. It SEEMED THAT
THE DESIre HAD FinAlly GOtten BiGGer ᵈⁿᵈ ᵗᴴᵉ ⁱⁿⁿᵉʳ ᶜʳⁱᵗⁱᶜˢ !
THAn THE EXCUSES AND THE FEArs.

For 2 WEEKS, I WroTE DAy AND
niGHT in MY MAGIC COttAGE, AND At THE
end, HAD no iDEA WHAT I HAD.

I SHOWED it very SHyly to THE
PUBlisHer, WHO SAID, "WE nEED to
PUBlisH THis—JUST AS it is." I WAS
GlAD, since I'D envisioned it With lots
OF Color, My HAnd Printing And Posters
inside. YⁿMMY, eccentric, Glowing With serendipity

A CrEAtive COMPAnion is now in its
tenTH Printing, And it lED to My
PUBlisHing A BOOK A yEAr since.

I MArvel At HOW BOOKS trAvel And
Move in THE WorlD And THrouGH lives.

I like to SAy tHAt A BOOK is like
A BiG letter to THE WorlD. IF you
WOUlD like to BE PUBlisHED, WHAT WOUlD
yOU like yOUr letter to SAy?

A
SHy
little
BooK

58

GLORY OF REJECTION

For ABOUT 12 years, everything I sent out into the world—my creative outpourings—was rejected.

My Art And words were sent BACK unreAD, or with terse little notes "not right For us" or somehow worse, "nice try But no!"

no no no no no NO!

It is very DiFFicult to continue Despite these rejections.

The one thing I heArD thAt kept me going WAs, "if you're not getting rejecteD, it meAns you're not reAching FAr enough."

This leD me to the concept of the glory of rejection. Let me tell you some of my FAvorite And most oDious rejections:

The Los Angeles Times sent my cArtoons BACK with a rejection letter TAPeD to the outside of the envelope—when I got BACK To The Hotel I lived in, Most of The stAff HAD reAD the letter!

The LonDon Times rejected my story, sAying, "We Don't Do inspirAtion."

The New Yorker said, "Your stuff is a bit too special for us."

There are so many more, most of them I blocked out or deliberately forgot.

My friend Larry says, "Why are you measuring how you feel by what you think you're not getting?"

But how can we continue along with the rejection?

By honoring and embracing rejection, by doing the creative work for the inside of us, not the reaction of the outside world.

By writing and speaking of rejection and what it means to us.

Remember your first dance? I was so terrified of rejection. Yet I was finally asked to dance and stared at my feet the whole time and hoped my deodorant was still working.

Arrid
extra
dry

Yes, it is much more pleasant to revel in the waves of acceptance and praise.

I used to worry about how I would handle book-signings, and a friend pointed out that I hadn't written a book yet!

We rush towards praise and turn away from rejection. We think rejection is "bad"

We reject ourselves and then project that onto the world. We blame whoever hasn't chosen us.

I have often felt a big stamp marked rejection land on my forehead.

Who hasn't applied for a loan, tried to get into a school, or lost a job?

We deal with various forms of rejection all the time. We think that "others" handle rejection better than us. They don't!

They don't!

61

PROMOTING THE GLORY OF REJECTION

HAVE JEALOUS OUTBURSTS: WHEN A FRIEND GETS AN ACCEPTANCE letter, or A GRANT, or into A JURIED SHOW, EXPress your JEALOUSY if you FEEL it! SHE KNOWS it ANYWAY. THEN YOU CAN BE HAPPY FOR HER.

Form A rejection CLUB: SHARE stories of rejection. CALL your CLUB to COMPLAIN AND receive support. THE telling lessens THE POWER.

A "CLUB" can Be any size or SHAPE

Collect rejection letters AND MAKE An AlBUM: SOMEDAY YOU CAN FLIP THROUGH THESE AND LAUGH. YOU CAN AlSO PUT THEM in A Fire, or SHARE THEM WITH A CREATIVELY STUCK FRIEND.

Dear ————.
your ———— is Actually not RIGHT FOR My work.
nice PUBLISHING try THO!
Hope you can STAY AFLOAT. GOOD luck.
————   THE CREATOR.

Write your own rejection letter To WHOever HAS rejected you! (YOU Can MAIL it or not. MOST of the ones I wrote were never MAILED, and were very SATISFYING too!)

REFUSE to BE STOPPED BY rejection! It CAN AlWAYS BE USED FOR MATERIAL lATER. SHARE THE HUMOR in rejection.   rejected

STUDYING FEELINGS

"THE THING TO DO WITH FEELINGS IS TO MAKE IT SAFE TO FEEL ALL OF THEM." ROBYN POSIN

We are endowed with these marvelous, complex, and simple things called feelings. We spend a lot of time trying not to have them, or having so many we can't function.

Most of us were not taught about healthy relationships with our feelings. We often hid our feelings, or our family system forbade us from even having them! In families without "feelings skills," it is common to react to feelings through explosive outbursts of anger. In my family, you were not allowed to have your feelings in front of others without being shamed or ridiculed.

The other option was to seek safety in isolation.

if you had a feeling, you went to your room to have it

Help
SADness
jealousy
SHAME
anger   stupid
Hopeless scattered lost
RAGE
anger

Keeping feelings bottled up only "works" temporarily

I didn't know how to navigate through the subtleties of feelings. I didn't know the rich layers of having more than one feeling at the same time, or just being honored for having feelings.

Now in my 40s, I am finally learning to claim my feelings as my own.

Hooray!

Studying feelings is a way to understand how they operate, where they come from, and how to hold them.

If we do not understand or allow our feelings, or have the ability to feel them, they can run our lives in a negative way.

We have the right to our feelings and can practice at letting them flow through us.

Feelings are marvelous gifts and can flow richly through us

"let others express their feelings. This way they can begin to process their beliefs."

JACQUELINE BIGAR

Gently Looking At Your Feelings

Begin To Draw, Color, or Write in These Bubbles — if you wish.

How were Feelings Held or Handled in your Family?

Have you ever kept a Feelings journal? How would you start?

Color your Feelings

is it safe for you to Feel?

What have you recently learned about Feelings?

I AM Feeling:

What are you Feeling right now?

Telling the Truth Faster

We are each keepers of our own truths. Sharing these truths opens doors for healing and intimacy with others. Still, we withhold the truth, fearing loss, or conflict, or judgment. We dance with deceptions and half-truths and hope we can evade "having to tell the truth."

We say, I couldn't tell the truth—I didn't want to hurt her feelings.

Yet "she" often knows or senses the truth anyway. So your lie leads to more lies and your truth is lost in the questions.

I often find it agonizing to tell or hear the truth, and will lie to myself to avoid knowing it. Professor Rita Barrecca calls these "enabling fictions." These lies to ourselves can build in layers until it is hard to even hear the truth.

"The present moment is a powerful goddess."

Goethe

66

My Brother Just told Me tHAt I AM A sedentAry person. My "enABLing Fiction" is tHAt I AM An AtHlete in My MinD, sure to stArt A ProgrAM At tHe gyM Any Minute...

The trutH is, I Do soMe stretCHing AnD MoDerAte WAlking on An interMittent BAsis. I'M A Binge exerCiser-every DAy or not At All. I WOULD like to CHAnge soMe of tHese pAtterns As I Age, PerHAps I Will or Won't, yet DeAling WitH tHe trutH Will serve Me Better tHAn My enABLing FiCtions.

We Also WitHHOLD trutH-telling in soMe DeMenteD HOPe tHAt tHe person Will Forget WHAt HAs HAPPeneD, or tHAt We Will Forget. There is so MUCH FreeDOM in Just sAying Our trutH-even if it is AWkWArD, or UnpleAsAnt, or BADly receiveD.

The outCOMe of tHe telling is not tHe point. We CAnnot ADJust our trutH ACCorDing to HOW tHe person Will respOnD. (Telling tHe trutH FAster) enABles Us to live More Freely, liGHtly, AnD POWerFULLy our-selves.

We Can DanCe our TrutHs

67

How can The TRUTH serve us?

If we live in truth, we will Be closer to our ACTUAl experience, And therefore, open to more joy, And more of our own essence. our essence selves love THe TruTH

The truth is our Ally And our revealer. If we let ourselves Be truly seen, then we CAn Be truly loved.

The truth HurTs And HEAls. Hurts when we FEAr And resist it, HEAls when we Allow it to spEAk And CHAnGe How we see.

TruTH QuesTions

Are you currently CHoosinG to lie?

ABOUT WHAT?

WHAT Are your rewArDs?

WHAT PART(s) Does TruTH PlAy in your LiFe?

WHAT lies seem essentiAl?

WHere can you increase TRUTH-TellinG?

Do you FEAr THe truTH?

How Do you explore THe truTH in your LiFe?

THe THrill oF THe TruTH

Jealousy
serves us

I wish we would all have more clear, truthfull, jealous outbursts. We all feel jealousy. I feel it often, about both odd and common things.

We are afraid that it is too ugly to be seen, or not kind, or some sign that we are greedy or inferior.

I AM so Jealous!

SAY THis wHen you feel it

If jealousy is shared consciously when felt, its power disappears. My friend Diane formed a "club" with another woman writer friend to share their jealousy about other writers "getting more."

Getting more is a big jealousy theme. We instantly forget what we have and temporarily want what seems better or more than we have.

If jealousy is not expressed, it shows up in all kinds of ways. Passive-aggressive questions, or thinly disguised fake "I'm really happy for you" speeches.

Trying to protect others from jealousy also occurs. We deny our own good fortunes for fear it will make another person jealous. We minimize or eliminate good news "just in case they're jealous."

"No, that's not a new car— it just looks new!"

This denies them their feelings, experience, and discounts their receptivity for more goodness.

and they'll find out your good news anyway!

Jealousy only points the way towards where we might like to go. It is a gift. an oddly wrapped gift

Jealousy increases in size if you feed it with silence. Practice saying loudly and firmly,

I AM so JEALOUS!

A woman came up to me after one of my events and said,
    "I'm afraid to say this, but I think you wrote my books. Now I feel like there are no more words left. I am so jealous of you."
She stood back and waited for my anger.
    I clasped her hands and said,

"I know that feeling exactly.
  I assure you that your words
  and books are waiting for you
  and that you'll be back to
  find them."
We feed jealousy with our
thoughts of scarcity:
        "There won't be enough
        left for me!"
        This is a big lie. **BIG**
But oh so tempting to believe!
        We collect evidence
        to make it true
        And drain our very lives
        of deserved rewards.

            We can stop it.

STOP

        Stop telling ourselves big lies and
        letting inner critics run our lives

72

learning ABOUT Jealousy

Do you ADMit your Jealousy when you feel it?

MAKE A list of ways you Get Jealous

Are you AWARe when others Are Jealous of you and can you HAVE A DiAlogue ABout it?

How was Jealousy HandleD, or spoken of, when you were Growing up?

Is THere someone you can ADMit Jealousy To right now? Can you Hear Hers/His?

READINGS:

THere is nothing wrong with you By Cheri Huber

Forgiveness and other Acts of love By Stephanie Dowrick

Sweat your prayers By Gabrielle Roth

CHecking in

Our emotional lives are messy and filled with half-expressed feelings, unexpressed needs, and withheld truths.

CHecking in is a simple way to navigate through feelings with others. You can simply (CHeck in) By asking the other person where she's traveled to in her mind, with any particular issue, and then explain where you are.

This is especially effective with projections- where we imagine our feelings are someone else's. Since projections happen in the mind, it is good to (CHeck in) and CHeck them out.

In this way, we can stay current with our emotions.

CHecking in can also save a lot of emotional time.

Check out your own projector!

You can agonize for a long time about what you think someone is feeling-without knowing.

Often, you can quickly check in and move on, or make a date to talk later.

I'm often amazed by how much movement can occur by checking in. So many times, I'm lost in my head, or projections, or fears and then I am not emotionally present.

We can receive support emotionally by checking in with those we care about.

Check in

Learning to check in with ourselves is another step towards emotional wholeness.

Excuse me, I need to check in with someone right now!

Group Therapy

I entered group therapy based on this description: "learning to be intimate with yourself in the presence of others."

Groups have often frightened me, or caused me to lose my emotional balance. I found myself "performing" for the group, or becoming someone else who I thought "they" would like better.

My girl scout troop was a group that I still have upsetting memories about. I frequently felt odd, left out, or not "in" somehow. I thought that other people just naturally knew "how to be" in a group. They don't!

I found out that a group can be a microcosm of your family of origin—that you can redo how you behaved and felt in that first primary group—your family.

How
Do
you
Feel
in
Groups?

THROUGH MY INDIVIDUAL THERAPY, I HAD LEARNED A LOT ABOUT INTIMACY WITH MYSELF—AND NOT AS MUCH ABOUT BEING MYSELF IN A GROUP.

I'VE SPENT 2 YEARS IN A THERAPY GROUP THAT IS VERY DEEP AND REAL. I WAS ABSOLUTELY TERRIFIED TO JOIN IT AND RESISTED AT EVERY MENTION OF IT.

NOW I WELCOME THE SUPPORT AND TRUTH-TELLING AND CHANCE TO BE MYSELF.

WE MEDITATE TOGETHER FOR A HALF HOUR BEFORE SPEAKING. IT IS SUCH AN HONOR TO SIT IN SILENCE IN A GROUP.

THE

HONOR

OF

SILENCE

OUR THERAPIST DESCRIBES THE GROUP AS A LABORATORY FOR A DEEPER LEVEL OF SOCIAL CONNECTION, AND A CHANCE FOR TRUE INTIMACY WITH ONESELF IN THE PRESENCE OF OTHERS. SOME OF US HAVE NOT YET FELT THAT. I AM NOW ABLE TO BE IN THE WORLD AS I AM IN GROUP... SOME OF THE TIME.

I'M STILL PRACTICING

How to Feel Like Yourself at a Party

One of the common groups we find ourselves in is a party. Some people avoid them entirely, others become someone else so they can go. Here's what I've learned:

Everyone at the party has issues with being at a party. There are very few party experts.

The party is made of the people who are at it. You are one of those people. It's ok to stay at a party for 5 minutes.

You can take party breaks and go outside or use the phone.

Call someone you love

It is not necessary to eat or drink at a party if you don't want to.

Speaking with other people can be fun or draining or just ok. Participate as you can, and then fall silent in the corner of a couch if you wish.

Hide on the couch

Parties do not have to be "fun." Sometimes the pressure to have fun takes all the fun away.

At a party, if you only connect with (one) person, let that person be (you.)

FACING CONFLICT

This is one of my "undeveloped countries." Conflict has been something I've hidden from, or headed straight towards, with no idea how to experience resolution.

With every relationship, personal or business, we experience conflict. Sometimes the friction from unexplored conflict ends relationships. We don't want to talk about it, or study it. We just hope it doesn't happen, or will go away.

Processing conflict is an art that contains gifts of expansion, strength, and joy.

JOY

Facing conflict truthfully requires trust, courage, and the willingness to hear another.

Conflict can teach us about our resilience and hopes for harmony. It can also reveal our defensiveness and paranoia.

We can learn to process conflict consciously

Our movements towards or away from conflict can show us where our lessons lie.

WHAT PART DOES CONFLICT PLAY IN YOUR LIFE?

HOW DO YOU HANDLE OR NOT HANDLE CONFLICT?

WHAT CAN YOU LEARN ABOUT CONFLICT?

WHEN HAVE YOU PROCESSED CONFLICT TO RESOLUTION?

HOW WOULD OTHERS DESCRIBE YOUR RELATIONSHIP WITH CONFLICT?

SOME WAYS TO HONOR CONFLICT

SPEAK OF IT. CONFLICT IS OFTEN A HIDDEN STRUGGLE.

STUDY IT. WRITINGS ON MEDITATION ARE HELPFUL.

REVEAL YOUR OWN CONFLICT PATTERN. WHERE DOES IT NEED WORK?

PROCESS IT WITH OTHERS. PRACTICE THIS ART. YOU WILL BE WELL REWARDED.

KEEP FACING IT. THE "TURNING AWAY" GIVES CONFLICT A HEAVINESS THAT ISN'T USEFUL.

I WISH FOR ALL OF US THE WILLINGNESS TO HAVE AND TO HONOR OUR CONFLICTS.

anGer
in All of its Disguises

I used to think I was most afraid of other people's anger. Now I think I'm more afraid of my own.

I am learning to work with my anger as it surfaces—or it leaps out! I'm afraid that my anger is too BiG or uncontained. I try to keep it in locked strongboxes inside, with elephants sitting on top to make sure it doesn't get out. of course it does!

the elephant is very kind to try and keep the anger from getting out, but usually there is a leak...

Other times, I just have outbursts and wonder where they came from.

WHAT PART Does anger play in your life? It is fascinating to explore your early anger models—your caregivers.

WHO GOT angry and why?

I wrote a poster called "How to Forgive your Father" and in it I say, "My DAD always got mad at Dinner — and I thought it was because of me so I sat up straight and tried to do it all perfect and He still yelled. His Dad got mad at Dinner too."

Anger follows generationally and patterns are set in motion before we're born that we Don't even realize.

There was a lot of anger and high levels of frustration in my family. Whenever my DAD tried to fix something, He got angry.

Many years later, I was Helping my Boyfriend put together a new Bed, and noticed How calm and quiet He was.

the CALM BED

WHen I ASkeD ABout it, He replieD THAT HIS DAD HAD Been CALM too. I WAS AlSo Witness to My Mother's RAGE anD Know THAT When I rAGe toDAY, I AM no DifferEnt.

anGer AvoiDance is very coMMon. we Control people anD situAtions in A MisGuiDED Attempt to "never Get anGry." People Also Don't use the worD anGry. InsteaD they sAy: upset, annoyed, irritAted. Sometimes, these Are Descriptive. often it is an Attempt to NOT Be anGrY.

person tries to SHIeLD FROM anGer

I've spent Many YeArS BeinG terrified of My own and others'anGer. we can leArn ABout anGer and How to Live succulently with it.

it's o.k. To Be anGry   83

Have you ever:

Been angry, told the person, and as you talked about it, forgotten that she has love for you and you for her?

Been angry and thought the whole relationship was over?

Abandoned yourself rather than feel the anger? Convinced yourself you're not angry, rather than face the other person?

Placated so that anger didn't even show up?

Lied when someone asked you if you were angry?

if you're human, you've probably done some or all of these.

WORKING with anGer

WHAT IS
your anGer style?
Describe it.

WHAT MAKES you anGry?

HOW Are you wHen others Are anGry?

WHO Got anGry As you Grew up? WHAT Did you Do?

in WHAT WAys HAs anGer HeAled or TAVGht you?

reADinGs:

THe Dance of anGer
        By Harriet Lerner

WHen THings FAll ApArT
        By PeMA CHöDrön

THe FeAr BOOK
        By Cheri HuBer

HoMecoMinG
        By JoHn BrADsHAW

Grudge Island

I keep saying I'm going to write a children's book titled <u>Grudge Island</u>. All the people on it would be bent over carrying the weight of all their grudges.

the sea of bitterness is deep and cold

In order to get there, you would have to swim through the sea of bitterness and once on Grudge Island, all you would do is sift through all your grudges.

Then I realized that the book idea is actually for me NOW and for anyone who spends time holding grudges.

GRUDGES DRAIN AWAY SUCCULENT LIVING.
If you ARE A GRUDGE-HOLDER, you spend
TIME sifting, counting, replaying, and
repeating.

THE EGO receives GREAT SATISFACTION
BY KEEPING GRUDGES. It Allows you to
BE RIGHT and to Live in the PAST.

Mostly, GRUDGES APPEAR with similar
energy and intensity AS WHEN the
incident occurred — no MATTER HOW
Many yEArs HAVE PASSED!

EVERY DAY COULD BE A GRUDGE OCCASION!

GRUDGE CALENDAR

GRUDGE CALENDAR						
1	2 THE Time...	3 Hurt	4	5 I remember	6	7
8 let me remind	9 THAT BAD DAY	10 you never...	11 He forgot to call	12	13	14
15 you of...	16 JUST in CASE	17 I'm right	18 you Always...	19 He's wrong	20	21 you Always
22 THE Time...	23 He DiDn't...	24 I remember	25 angry AT...	26 She DiDn't...	27	28 still angry

GRUDGES
Are Companions
of struggle
and BLAME.
Sometimes we
FeeL it's Better to HAve their Company
than none AT All, so we continue
letting THEM Live and Grow.

87

I'M STILL HOLDING GRUDGES FROM CHILDHOOD, and FROM LAST WEEK. GRUDGES BECOME STUCK and FROZEN IN OUR CONSCIOUSNESS. (note: THIS is DIFFERENT THAN JUST CONTINUING to FEEL THE PAIN FROM SOMETHING THAT HAPPENED IN THE PAST.)

We can HELP EACH OTHER WAKE UP.

FIND SOMEONE YOU KNOW WHO HOLDS GRUDGES and WISHES to CHANGE THIS PATTERN. SEE IF SHE'LL PLAY A GRUDGE GAME WITH YOU. WHEN SHE HEARS YOU REPEATING A GRUDGE, or SEE THAT YOU ARE STUCK IN HOLDING A GRUDGE, SHE'LL REPEAT SOME WORD OR SIGNAL YOU'VE AGREED ON to BREAK THE "SPELL."

AT LEAST, it WILL BRING NEW AWARENESS to THIS PATTERN.

MY FRIEND BRIGETTE USED to JUST QUIETLY SAY THE WORD "BITTER" WHEN SHE WOULD HEAR ME or SOMEONE ELSE BEING IT.

SOMETIMES WE'RE SWIMMING IN A TINY LITTLE PATTERN

BITTER

I plan on spending much more time on pleasure island, surrounded by the sea of changes.

pleasure island is full of LOVE

MAGIC and eccentric houses

THE SEA OF CHANGES IS ALWAYS DIFFERENT

GRUDGE reminders:

☆ GRUDGE rhymes with sludge.

☆ GRUDGES have a repetitive quality to them, and usually involve some form of the "angry victim."

☆ The GRUDGE-keeper is often not taking responsibility for her part in keeping the GRUDGE GAME going.

Let's swim together in the sea of changes, and put our attention in the present and towards our own souls.

DEATH
TOUCHES US ALL

I WAS surprised to discover HOW many people would rather not talk about death. For me, sharing stories of death is one of the best ways to navigate through it.

"The doctors" wouldn't actually say that my dad was dying—but we knew it. That year at Christmas, we were visiting my parents and there in the kitchen, I saw a man I didn't recognize. He had on a plaid bathrobe and was hunched over, lurching around the corner, gasping for breath. He was an old dying man, and he was my father.

MY DAD looked GOOD in PLAID

I'D been preparing, rehearsing, and practicing for his death since prostate cancer was discovered 5 years before.

Then he told me, "Honey—I'm worried about you. I'm going to die, and you need to be able to live with that."

I don't know how he knew I wasn't "ready" but he did. That year he died, I sat in the car with him in a cold parking lot in Minneapolis, and told him, "Dad, I thought a lot about what you said about your death, and you were right, I wasn't ready. I want you to know that as much as I don't want you to <u>ever</u> die, I'm ready now—and if you need to go, I'll be ok."

Somehow, I felt I was in a state of grace about his death.

He went into hospice care a few months later and we shared "I love yous" on the phone.

i love you   i love you too

Several DAys lAter, He sAid tHAt He "WAsn't Doing too Well" But tHAt it WAs up to me WHen to go tHere. I WAs sick tHAt nigHt, AnD DeciDeD to WAit until tHe next DAy to trAvel.

THAt nigHt I slept WitH tHe Beeper on tHAt I'D gotten so I coulD Be reAcHeD At All times. eArly tHAt next morning, tHe Beeper Went off, AnD I leApt out of BeD like some kinD of firefigHter, AnD cAlleD my MotHer. SHe sAiD, "I DiDn't pAge you, AnD tHe Hospice DiDn't eitHer, BecAuse I Just spoke WitH tHem AnD your fAtHer is ok."

THe angeL Beeper

THese Were tHe only 2 people WHo HAD tHe Beeper number.

During tHAt conversAtion WitH my mom, tHe Hospice cAlleD to sAy, "you'D Better come noW."

THe Beeper mystery WAs never solveD

I got the very first flight from San Francisco to Minneapolis and sobbed almost the whole way. I had never been that emotionally naked in public before, and there was some kind of wild relief in it.

I was horrified that there were no phones on the plane, and we were delayed on the ground for almost an hour by a big thunderstorm. All I could think of was getting there, and I finally cried myself into some kind of stuporous sleep.

it seemed like the weather exactly matched my mood

When I woke up, it was to see the sun slanting in the window, and I felt extraordinarily calm and rested. In that instant, I knew that my father had died.

When I got off the plane, I found my brother there

shaking his head and saying,
  "He didn't make it."
   He had died at the same time
the sun had come in the window.
   I went instantly to a flower
cart and bought the brightest
bouquets they had, and called the
hospice to make sure that they
would hold his body until I got
there. I am still so gratefull for that hospice care

   I'd never seen a dead body,
and I knew I didn't want to see
it in a morgue or mortuary. I also
knew that if I didn't see that he
was dead, I wouldn't believe that
he _was_ dead.
   I entered the room that felt
like it would change my life
forever.
   My mom stood bravely there, and
the kind hospice people floated
94 around.

There was my dad, in flannel pajamas—clearly dead. It was true. The body is just this big container. The spirit was so clearly gone.

My mother squeezed his foot through the covers and said, "46 years of fun with this guy..."

At the same time, I was holding his hand, and didn't realize that her holding his foot would make his body move, and I jumped with fear. My mother said, "Oh, you are just cracking up!" And I replied,

"Mom, This is where you crack up. At the bedside of your dead father. It's ok to 'crack up.' We're all cracking up right now."

"It is through the cracks in our brains that ecstasy creeps in."
Logan Pearsall Smith

In the Midwest, it is common to not show your real feelings, or to not get "too out there." I was never more certain of the validity of my feelings as I was at that moment.

I also had to laugh that we were squabbling over my dad's dead body. He hated arguments and always tried to stop them.

Oddly now, we were free of that, and my father was free of his human container.

None of the preparation I'd done really worked after his death. The grieving and recovery continue. We write our own Healing Guidebooks

Presence is all that applies— being present for my actual experience and feelings.

AnD so I HAve Been iniTiATeD into
THe DeATH ClUB. It's A FunnY kinD
OF CluB-DeATH is THe entry AnD
THere Are no rUles. It is
imPossiBle to imAGine THe effects
OF A DeATH in ADvAnce.
    every insTAnt HAs A new
Precious kernel now: THe
AwAreness OF oUr HorriBle AnD
tenDer FrAGility-oUr Brief livinG AnD
THe immense mysteries.
    My mom sAiD,
    "Well, He's GoinG to Be DeAD A
     lonG time."
    AnD so Are we All.
How can we Live sUccUlenTLy wiTH THe Dying?

        "WHere THere is rUin,
         THere is HoPe For
         A TreAsure."
                        RUMI

Living with Dying

WHO DIES? WHO HAS DIED IN YOUR LIFE?

HOW HAS DEATH TOUCHED OR HEALED YOU?

WHAT ARE YOUR WORST FEARS ABOUT DEATH?

ARE THERE WAYS YOU AVOID DEATH? DO YOU TALK ABOUT IT?

WHAT WOULD YOUR TOMBSTONE OR OBITUARY SAY TODAY?

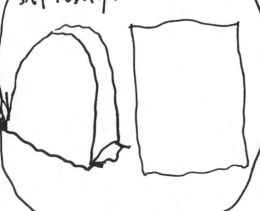

READINGS:

A YEAR TO LIVE STEPHEN LEVINE

WISDOM OF NO ESCAPE PEMA CHÖDRÖN

THE ESSENTIAL RUMI Translations BY Coleman BARKS WITH JOHN MOYNE

YOU'RE NOT OLD UNTIL YOU'RE NINETY... REBECCA LATIMER

PATHS OF HEALING

"EMBRACE YOUR GRIEF, FOR THERE YOUR SOUL WILL GROW."
JUNG

I AM AlWAYS WANTING HEAlinG TO OCCUR in A StrAiGHt line, or in SOME KinD OF "COnnect tHe DOts" MAP.

SOME PArt OF ME is AlSO AlWAYS COUnting— the nUMBer OF MOntHs Since MY FAtHer's DEAtH, tHe nUMBer OF yEArs Since I SPOKE WitH MY OlDer BrOtHer, HOW lOnG it's Been Since I SPOKE WitH SOMEOne FrOM yEArs PASt, FrOM A FrienDSHiP tHAt's enDeD.

IF Only HEAlinG tOOK PlAce in SOME KinD OF reASOnABle PAttern! THe SEDUctiOn OF tHis PAttern is tHe iDEA tHAt I COUlD PrEDict, reHEArse, or COntrOl tHe OUtcOME (Or At lEASt FEEl liKE it).

I tHinK tHOUGHtS liKE,

"After more than a year since my father's death, I should be feeling _____."

I believe healing happens in spirals and layers and inside interior crevices. It comes at 4AM while watching the moon, or at a dinner party where someone looks like your lost loved one.

My own healing from sibling incest has taken years of trust-building and monster-dismantling. New pockets of pain still materialize in my relationships with myself and others from years past.

Shrinking the Monsters

I am larger than this pain

Now I know that I am larger than this pain, I can experience more self-love daily.

HEALING DOESN'T CARE ABOUT THE YEARS, OR ABOUT THE COUNTING. I THINK IT IS TIMELESS AND WITHOUT AGE. IT WAITS FOR OUR SOULS TO SHIFT INTO ACCEPTANCE.

"YOUR SOUL IS HUNGRY FOR MOIST, RICH COMMUNION."

ROB BREZSNY

I WISH FOR YOU:
THE WILLINGNESS TO LOOK RIGHT AT THE SADDEST PARTS OF YOURSELF AND ALLOW HEALING TO TAKE PLACE.

TO THINK OF YOURSELF AS COMMITTED TO HEALING IN YOUR AND OTHERS' LIVES.

TO EXPLORE HEALING IN NEW AND UNFAMILIAR WAYS.

"I WANt to Know if you've
touched the center of your own
sorrow, if you've Been opened
By life's BetrAyAls, or HAve
Become shriveled And closed
From FeAr of Further pAin."
                              White Crow

  We Are All in vArious stAtes or
stAGes of HeAlinG. let's
reMEMBer this As others FAlter
or FAll or APPeAr to Be Acting
stupidly.
    let's pick eAch other up, Drive
More slowly And Kindly, And Be
conscious of JUDGinG And its
HArM to ourselves And others.

We Are All illuMinAteD From Within

YOUR HEALING MAP

WHAT IS CURRENTLY "UP FOR HEALING" IN YOUR LIFE?

BODY
WHAT IS IT SAYING?

SPIRIT
HOW IS IT SPEAKING?

relationships (others)
WHAT ARE THEY SHOWING YOU?

relationship (self)
WHAT ARE YOU SAYING TO YOU?

MIND
WHAT'S IN THERE FOR HEALING?

readings and resources

LEGACY OF THE HEART
BY WAYNE MULLER

THE
SEXUAL HEALING JOURNEY
BY WENDY MALTZ

SHARE THE CARE: HOW TO ORGANIZE A
GROUP TO CARE FOR SOMEONE WHO IS SERIOUSLY
ILL
BY CAPPY CAPOSSELA
AND SHEILA WARNOCK

FILM: · resurrection
· Cross creek
· OLD MAN

103

ving More succulently
(I have no idea)

"...are put on earth a little space that we might learn to bear the beams of Love." —William Blake

What am I thinking of, writing about love? My own love abilities feel so feeble and incomplete. I know that I love, yet I am consistently disappointed with how I show love. Perhaps my stumblings can inspire. *I hope so*

I spend a large percentage of my love life being beseiged by my inner critics. letting your inner critics into your love life is a horrible experience. everything you do will be torn apart and held up to some perfect ideal of what you have heard and read that love should be. *Tangled can be untangled*

It can be tangled and uncertain.

This is my work, to learn how to love and be loved.

this is what I <u>know</u> about loving succulently.

Here are some ways that work for me:

learn to FiGHT your inner Critics As Fiercely As you would an Attacker. The inner critics Started For A GOOD purpose When we were SMAll and Grew out of proportion to WHAT we need NOW.
learning to stop inner critic AttACKS is essential For Love to Grow.

Keep surprise close At HanD. I often criticize Myself and The Man I Love. THe other niGHT, AS I WAS listing His FAULts in My MinD, I SUDDenLy CALLeD Him to "Meet Me on The BACK StAirs, HALfWAy Down." He SOUnDeD QUite touCHeD By My sUGGestion.
I DiDn't even Know WHY. But I SomeHoW Knew THAT if We stood in The SUMMer WinD and MooN Together, SoMething COULD SHiFT. AND it DiD.

Be WilLing To Live inBetween riGHT and WronG. THe eGo needs and Desperately Wants to Be riGHT and Make others WronG. In Between riGHT and WronG is A soft, Messy, LAUGHing plAce WHere it Doesn't MAtter.
I'M still spenDinG an inorDinAte AMount of time trying to Be riGHT.
THere is MUCH to leArn.

105

(WAKE UP to LOVE.) Most of us Are Asleep without even knowing it. Love is A Conscious process of truth·telling and SOUL-SHARING. Be AWAKE FOR WHAT POPS UP.

It is very tempting to Distance, or DisAppear, or Hide From The Broken places and Deeper lAyers of Love.

ULTiMAtely, THis Doesn't WORK·

(Love imperfectLy.) Be A Love iDiot. Spill things. Tell secrets. let yourself FORGEt any Love "iDeAL" or comparison. Be Mis·SHAPen.

WAKE Up LAUGHing and cry FreQuently For no reAson. perfection in Love is A NArrow AND Suffocating pAtH.

I can Attest to the nuMBiNG, unrewArDiNG effects of it in Love.

PleAse Surrender to Love. Let Love in PAST All your ArMor.

Let Love FLOW PAST All the FloODGAtes · FLOAT in the ArMs of Love.

I AM often consumed by resisting surrender and trying to re-direct love. I AM opening to more surrender.

Be inspired By Trust. over and over, I forget that I AM loved and loving. I AM often sure that I will Be discovered as an unlovable fraud. Do not trust this. Trust only love.

Turn your FACE towards love and find the Dancing part of your ♡ HEART. ♡ ♡♡ ♡ ♡ ♡ ♡ ♡ ♡ Welcome the DARK parts of love and the Deep, unknown layers. let them speak too.

swim in the swirl of love love with all your faucets on. We are gifted in love even if we Dont know how yet. I'll see you in the caves of Discovery.

"Be patient toward all
that is unsolved in your
heart and try to love the
questions themselves like
locked rooms and like books
that are written in a very
foreign tongue. Do not now
seek the answers, which cannot
be given you because you would
not be able to live them. And
the point is, to live everything.
Live the questions now.
Perhaps you will then gradually,
without noticing it, live along
some distant day into the answer."

RAINER MARIA RILKE

reALLove stories

Love is messy, inconvenient, and often annoying. This is not spoken of enough.

When you are single, it is tempting to GAZE AT couples longingly and wonder, "Why not me?" When you are part of a couple, sometimes you look at single people and wonder, "When can I do that again?"

Being in Love is Not Better. It is Different.

reAL Love stories are what people hide. They tell about romantic moments and exaggerate how much FUN love is.

Here are some reAL love stories:

Sometimes you sleep next to your loved one and wake up hundreds of times, for noise, or just the newness of it. You spend the next day barely awake wondering if you will ever get some sleep. We all cling to our sleep habits

You're at a restaurant together and cannot decide what to order. your loved one is impatient and tries to hurry you. You order something that gives you a stomach-ache and you spend most of the night blaming this one you love. Menu of choices

You go away for a "romantic weekend" and are crushed by the expectations of it— yours or his. You spend the majority of the time arguing.

Oh no! The pressure to have fun

Both of you agree to (HAVE MORE FUN) together, and have disagreements about what the "fun" should be.

Real love stories can tilt other ways too.

You and your partner haven't been getting along very well, and you get together to "talk about it." Instead, you lie down in tall grass together and share a night of appreciation for each other. There in the grass you see essence

You meet to go shopping or do errands, and it turns into an unexpected walking adventure and you laugh all night.

One of you gets sick and you pile all the pillows and blankets into a fort and watch endless bad tv movies together (or really good old tv movies).

During a long car trip, you see the sun on your lover's face and feel an overwhelming wave of love. Waves of love are important

. All of these real love stories involve being alive and succulent in the moment. Sometimes we have pictures in our heads of what we think love is, or what it looks like.

Yet love lives in the moments that are unplanned and beyond our control.

If we can just feel our way from one real moment to the next, we will be living our love story.

Your real love story is All Around you IN A MAGnificent SWiRL

N   O   W.

We can love ourselves the way we wish To Be loveD.

WHAT Kind of love story Are you living?

Fear of Love

Love songs And love stories
Do not speak enough (or At All)
About the times you will hAte your
loved one, And be AfrAid of love
itself. we WOULD rAther not think of such things

TrAvel is A very
GOOD PlAce to bring up
MAny of these feelings.
How A person trAvels is full of
PlAces to be Annoyed, irritAted,
And fed up. I remember
trAveling in europe with this MAn
And thinking thoughts like, "IF I
HAve to look At the <u>BACk</u> <u>of</u> <u>his</u>
<u>STUPID</u> <u>HEAD</u> for one more DAy..."

FEAR
OF LOVE

A
lot of
feeLings
cAn get
projected
onto the
bAck of
A heAd

eAting is Another
PlAce to explore
these emotions.

The way someone chews or swallows can elicit very strong primitive responses, leading to questions like,

"Do you have to chew like that?" or, "is it necessary to GULP?"

My friend John calls these things the "nuance of annoyance." How many ways can another person annoy us and what is it really saying?

"When you find yourself JUDGING someone... look for what in yourself you are not yet willing to accept... Hold that part of you more gently!"

roByn Posin

For Robyn Posin's soul-full cards & catalog, call 805·646·4518 or write: Box 725 Ojai CA 93024

Since love brings up everything unlike itself, and magnifies areas of dysfunction in ourselves, it is a ripe place to experience hatred, annoyance, and fear.

Fear of love is a very real thing. People are often afraid to receive what they really want in love, maybe because then they'll be trapped by love? It's a paradox.

"open your arms and embrace paradox."

Marion Woodman

I'm practicing at allowing the fear of love to exist as it comes up. Feeling the feelings and knowing they are matters of the ego and persona, we can move into essence, where fear has no place.

NO VACANCY

read Marion Woodman books - they're deep & true

read The Fear Book by Cheri Huber

We fear loss of love, loss of control, being overwhelmed by another. We assume we should just Know How to love.

Yet we often don't know how to love ourselves, so when we are fully met in love, we question it by saying, "AM I lovable?" or, "AM I worthy of this love?"

YOU Are LovABle Yes.

It is difficult to receive love if you are caught in feelings of unworthiness.

Fear of love is often a hidden dilemma. It is much more romantic and acceptable to speak about the wonders of love, the glory of love— yet we must also speak about the fear of love.

WORKING WITH THE FEAR of LOVE

Do you ever feel the Fear of Love? How?

WHAT Are you Most Afraid of About Love?

In WHAT WAYs Do you Hide From Feeling even More Love?

I'm NOT Afraid of love BECAUSE...

READINGS

BECOME THE PERSON you want To Find CHeri HuBer

He, SHe, owning your SHADOW RoBert Johnson

ADDICTION To perfection MARion WOODMAN

THE CONSCIOUS HEART KATHLyn & GAy HenDricks

eMBRACING ourselves HALSSIDrA STONE

OPEN BODY TODD WALTON, DrAWINGS By VINCE LAWRY

Love Support

Who supports you in love? Who do you share the scary, marvelous, tumultuous feelings of love with? This includes self-love.

Do you have support when love is and isn't working?

Conscious loving is a lot of work. Some of this work involves facing parts of the self that we don't necessarily want to see or experience.

I get scared of the angry parts of my self

I am currently learning how to be part of a team with my partner.

When conflict arises, or feels too thick, I often just quit the team, and stop participating.

I'm often mentally "breaking up" with my lover, just to try and find what feels like safety. Some part of me thinks that if I can just get rid of him, I'll be "back in control."

My ego whispers seductively,

"It was easier when you were alone..."

It is possible to use books and tapes, form couples groups, or participate in free co-counseling sessions. There are many kinds of support and you can invent your own kind.

Since I'm involved in both couples therapy and group therapy, I usually get a new perspective and orientation with which to proceed.

There are many types of couples therapy to explore. Most of all, it means you have a witness to your relating.

new point of view

119

We All need super.Vision: someone
to Help us steer our relationship
craft, or to provide us with
maps on where there are
shallows and riptides.

love

Our craft of
Love is festive
and elegant...
with barnacles
too!

I was terrified to
start couples therapy,
yet I was more
terrified of not trying.

I was afraid of exposure, of
being made wrong, of being
"ganged up on" by my partner and
therapist, of the therapy
uncovering unsolvable problems
and causing us to break up.

Breaking
up

even though we've just
started couples therapy, All of
the above has already happened
in some form.

Yet something much richer Also
happened.

I DiscoVereD HOW MUCH love I HAVe For My PArtner, AnD HOW MUCH He loves Me. I sAW it cleArly in Front of the therApist, AnD I Felt it very strongly in the rooM.

   This HAs Given Me new FAith AnD courAGe When the PAth is scAry AnD UncleAr.

SOMe TiMes THe PATH is so uncertAin it AppeArs To Be DAnGerous

"IF GOD senDs Us on strong PAths We Are ProviDeD strong shoes."

                    corrie TenBOOM

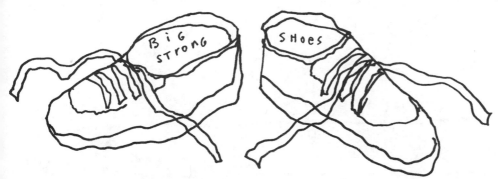

BIG STRONG SHOes

WAYS TO Support Love

How is your love AFFAir with your (self)?

WHo Do you SHARE stories of Love with?

is it nourishing?

Are you now, or could you Be, in A Group THAT supports love? WHAT could it Be Like?

Do you Feel your love relationship (self & others) works well? How could it work Better?

We CAn let light And new iDeAs into our love relAtionships. We CAn tell tHe trutH And ADMit WHere love is And isn't WorKing.

TrutH HeAls

We CAn Know We Are not Alone.

Succulent Wild Men

Men Are not the Problem.
I see men's shoulders come down
About a foot when I say that. As
A woman who has been sexually and
physically abused by men, I continue
now to find safety and understanding
with men who do not hurt women—and
there are so many more of these.

Men Are Also yearning for
succulence. They Are crying,
fumbling, dreaming, seeking, and
healing too.

They Are releasing their neckties
and refusing to leave their children
and families for work.

Men Are blooming,
changing, and growing
into more self-Love.

and their neck ties became birds and flew
away...

I USED to DreAM ABOUT A
SOciety WiTH no Men.
    now I DreAM ABOUT the loving
Men And WoMen WHo DAre to
Cross long PlAces of
MisUnDerstAnDing to Meet
GrAteFully in the MiDDle.
        G r A T e F u l l y in THe MiDDle

 "oUt BeyonD iDeAs of
   WronGDoing AnD riGHtDoing
              tHere is A FielD.
           I'll Meet you there."

                                    rUMi

I WANt to Honor My Men FrienDs WHo
Are not ProFileD in tHis BooK:
   the BrilliAnt JoHn G. The enDeAring AnD
inDeliBle LArry R. The^Deluxe FAiry GoDFATHer
George. The UncoMMon MAx. The electric
Brett. The FAvorite Roy. The GiFteD
LArry T. THe Wise GAry. The KinD JoHn H.
THe eleGant Victor. THe WArM TAKis. To THe MeMory
let's PAy triBUte to All the excellent
Men We love AnD Know!

In MeMory of My FAtHer, ArT KenneDy, WiTH WHoM I'D BeGUn An ADUlt FrienDsHip.

Joe

Joe channels the spirit
of my cat, Jupiter. Joe
can be found slinking
behind bookshelves, or
curled in a big chair, purring.
    He was a journalist with a major
newspaper for 15 years, but left to
follow his dreams of living in San
Francisco and living more succulently.
    He's been arranging flowers, waiting
tables and catering, and continuing his
various practices of meditation and
spirituality. Joe says, "I still haven't
found what I'm looking for — but that is
part of the journey."
    Joe had concerns that perhaps he
wouldn't be as interesting without the
job as a journalist. I said to him,
    "you could be sitting in a tiny
room on a stool in your underwear and
still be captivating on all levels."

I love watching people melt around him. His engaging spirit, gorgeous smile, and welcoming heart are a joy to know.

Photos of Joe and me at 10 years old were so similar, that it seemed very clear we were once childhood friends in some other lifetime, or that the children inside of us love each other now.

Joe is brilliantly creative, wistful, and magnetic.

He can also be hidden, evasive, and emotionally distant and turbulent.

When I first met him, over a huge bowl of fresh raspberries in Big Sur, he smiled shyly and said,

"Is it you?"

We grinned at the instant old friendship between us. He is one of my favorite succulent men.

Ken

I call Ken's voice "the rolls royce of voices."

Man in radio

He's in radio, and it's a good thing, because he has a famous radio voice.

Ken is also stunningly funny, loud, and romantic. He adores his wife, Adrienne, and is such

He also likes her-which is a rare combination

an inspiration as a father to Zoe (age 3).

Ken stayed on the late-night shift at his radio job for the first 3 years of Zoe's life, so he could spend most of each day with her.

His devotion and utter commitment to fathering is breathtaking for me and others to see. **B**reathtaking

Kenny is a profoundly loving man who radiates kindness. I feel very lucky to be one of his dear friends. When I think of my friendship with Ken, I am immediately reminded of his heart-full, great hugs. Ken also coaches me on my audiotapes, and stands just outside the studio window, making me laugh and giving me such confidence. For years, Ken was my 3 am phone friend when he also worked late nights, and there were many times his calls kept me creatively going. Ken's voice is an elixir

Ken and I share truth-telling, discussions of love and life, and process feelings as they come up.

Ken is very energetic and, as an only child, sometimes doesn't know how rough he plays and his teasing

so much laughter...

sometimes goes too far and isn't funny.

I see Ken working through past resentments and grudge-holding from his past, and I see his openness to processing feelings as they come up.

He is sometimes extra sensitive to perceived criticism and quick to anger. I am proud of him for letting me share this about him!

Ken formed his own company called Radio Partners, which handles voice talent and audio production. He has an in-home studio, and produces shows and commercials there.

Ken's basic goodness and lack of guile are very refreshing to be around. He is such a male, yet his female side is highly developed, and I feel profoundly safe around him.

I think of Ken as my "other brother" and treasure his existence.

CRAIG
MCNAIR
WILSON

MCNAIR is THE MOST
CREATIVE PERSON I
KNOW, AND POSITIVELY
BULGES WITH TALENT.

He is ALSO ENDEARING,
CLEVER, SMART, FUNNY, AND
WISE. SINCE I'M IN LOVE WITH HIM, THIS
WILL BE A SLIGHTLY TILTED PORTRAIT. I
WILL PRETEND TO BE OBJECTIVE.

SLIGHTLY TILTED

MCNAIR is ALSO THE MOST ANNOYING
PERSON I CAN THINK OF. He is OFTEN
IMPATIENT, JUDGMENTAL, AND CAN BE
SCATHINGLY SARCASTIC. Yet I PREFER
TO FOCUS ON ALL THE GOODNESS I SEE IN
HIM. AS I BECOME HIS BEST FRIEND, I
SEE MORE AND MORE OF HIS **H**UGE HEART
GREAT BIG HEART.

AMONG MANY OTHER THINGS, He is A
CHRISTIAN REPUBLICAN. THESE 2
DESCRIPTIONS TERRIFIED ME BEFORE I

met him, And continue to FAscinAte And puzzle me As we grow in love together. I Discovered thAt I WAs Filled with stereotypes About Christians And republicAns, And had never reAlly Given either A CHAnce. We HAD endless Discussions About WHAt we ActuAlly Believe, insteAd of cAteGories. it is so tempting to form rights and wrongs

His FAith is A BeAutiful thing thAt I respect. He welcomes my skepticAl questions And HAs mAny of his own. I found moderAtion in his politics, And Discovered thAt we Agree on much more thAn I would HAve imAGineD. DiD I SAy enough About how Funny he is?

I cAll McNAir obstreperous—An upstArt—And I know thAt he delights in turning viewpoints inside out And upside Down. Unlike me, he welcomes rAtionAl Discussion About most subjects And is FAirly open to chAnGing his mind. (FAirly open...)

I feel fully met By him—he is mostly present in mind And spirit, And sometimes we dance in our bodies too.

He is a Christian activist—I call him the "Christian Robin Williams," yet he is truly a magnificent original, with his 2 one-man plays he performs all around the country.

He was an Imagineer with Disney for 10 years and now has his own company called Imaginuity Unlimited. He helps teach people and companies to be more creative. I am very inspired by him, and by his abundant, incredibly funny mind.

McNair is also a writer, with one published book and many more in various stages of completion.

look for Raised in Captivity

He acts, directs, draws, paints, creates, and is an outstanding napper and sleeper too! Thank heavens he can sleep! otherwise I might be crushed by "Activity Man."

We are each other's biggest fans—and it is a sheer joy for me to just be Susan—the woman he loves.

anDrew JoHn KenneDy

I WAS 11 WHen AnDrew WAS Born, AnD I DelighteD in FeeDing HiM AnD CHAnGing His DiAPers. now He's 32, AnD I someTimes sAy tHAt I useD to CHAnGe His DiAPers.

AnDrew will rePly,

"not recently."

AnDrew is A stuDent, HistoriAn, sCHolAr- witH A GreAt BiG iMMense HeArt. THere is A rADiAtinG GooDness ArounD HiM tHAt is very enDeArinG.

WHen I sAiD tHAt I WAnteD to inCluDe tHis PortrAit oF HiM As A suCCulent MAn, He WAS DouBtFul ABout WHAt I MiGHt write.

"I don't know if I've done anything succulent yet in my life," he said.

In his late twenties, Andrew moved to California and started over in college, from the beginning. I watched him join the community college swim team where his teammates affectionately called him "the old fat bald guy" because he has a receding hairline and slightly more body fat than 9%. He was also a decade older than the other guys, yet he beat most of them at swim times. it's really fun to watch Andrew swim!

He won't speak of his grades except to say, "I did well enough to continue." But let me say as his proud older sister, that he did just about as well as you can do.

After 2 years at a community college, he got into U.C. Berkeley, and after one successful semester, went home to help our father die.

He nursed both parents, and helped run the household. After our dad died, he stayed on for a year to help our mother. In doing this, he lost his residency status at school. This delay was another frustration for a 32-year-old undergraduate. My Brother is Brave and kind

To me, this is sheer succulent living and I wish to honor a kind and sensitive man in our world. He is truly one of those "nice guys" that aren't spoken of enough. let's speak of them more!

Andrew is also single-minded, argumentative, stubborn, somewhat volatile, and a procrastinator. (I can list more faults because I said so many good things.)

I am often the recipient of Andrew's understanding and solid, steady, and loving ways.

We are friends as well as siblings, and I am so glad he is one of my best friends.

P.S. He's single.

Jupiter

I first met Jupiter in the window of a department store, where he was up for adoption.

Before long, I had become one of those "cat people." How could they love a cat so much? Now I know. They teach us all about unconditional love

I credit Jupiter with paying my rent because he discovered my poster "How to Be an Artist" by carefully tearing it off the wall every day until I paid attention! The poster went on to sell many many hundreds of thousands of copies.

Jupiter is an adventure to know and live with. He eats paper and knows how to play without using claws. He only knows 2 tricks: A back flip where I hold him in the

Beginning position, upside down, facing away, and he pushes off backward into a flip, and something I invented called "earthquake discovery," where I put a bunch of pillows over my face and call for help. Jupiter jumps on my loft bed and digs through the pillows until he uncovers my face. Handy in an earthquake!

He knows how to take crackers off the shelf and eat them for a snack, he is a telepathic communicator, and I certainly have learned about unconditional love from him.

Jupiter has a very loud purr and adores me. He is also relentless for playtime and is very vocal and stubborn.

Jupiter is a grand spirit guide.

Jupiter draws love

SABRINA WARD HARRISON

SABRINA CALLED MY inspiration phone line And DESCRIBED THAT HAViNG MONO HAD HAlteD HeR life, THAt SHE WAS "DiSHeveleD AND UNcertAin, PAle AND itCHy."
I CAlleD HeR BACK to tHANk HeR FOR BEiNG WilliNG to BE DiSHeveleD AND to SPEAK OF it.

SOON I WAS SPEAKiNG OF MY FeeliNGS WitH HeR AND WE lAUGHED AS OUR NEW friendSHiP WAS BOrn.

SABRinA is 22 yeArs old, eleGANt, DEEPly CreAtive, AND FUll OF WAKING DREAMS. THere SEEMS to BE StArDUSt NEAr HER, ABUNDAnt vUlnerABility, AND tOUCHiNG HUMANity.

WHEN I First SAW HER JOUrNAls, I SAW volUMES OF BOOKS inSide tHEM. SHE is BOTH Artist AND AUtHOr As Well AS life explorer.

SABrinA's PArents Are HiGHly
CreAtive, sensitive souls. Her
FAtHer is An inspired FilMMAker, Her
Mother A Gifted CoMMuniCAtor
Between PArents And CHildren.

   IF I'D HAD A sister or DAuGHter,
I would HAve WAnted Her to Be like
SABrinA.

   It is DiFFiculT to speAk oF
SABrinA's FAults or FIAws, since I
AM rAtHer Protective oF Her, But
the PortrAit MAy not Be CoMPlete
WitHout A Few sHADOW Points.

   SABrinA's CAIM soMetiMes
DisGuises Anger, And Her tendency
to "Blend in" is soMetimes Annoying
WHen you JUst WAnt to HeAr Her reAl
experience. Her ethereAl QUAlities
CAn Be FrustrAtinG WHen you JUst
WAnt the BAsic person. AnD THe "BAsiC person" is so GreAt

   Since sHe is AviDly DOinG Her OWn
PsyCHOlOGiCAl Work, I trust Her to   139

SPEAK OF ANY OTHER FLAWS.

SABRINA IS A STUDENT AT THE CALIFORNIA COLLEGE OF ARTS AND CRAFTS, AND RECENTLY BEGAN TEACHING ART AND DISCOVERY AT PRIVATE SCHOOLS AND TO INDIVIDUALS (OF THE CHILD VARIETY).

SHE HAS ALSO JUST SIGNED HER FIRST (OF MANY!) BOOK CONTRACT, AND IS WORKING FROM HUNDREDS OF INDEX CARDS TAPED TO THE WINDOWS OF HER FANTASTIC STUDIO-BEDROOM-PORCH-ARTSPACE-TREEHOUSE-HOME.

look for SABRINA WARD HARRISON's BOOK IN OCTOBER 1998!

SABRINA'S CREATIVE SPACE IS A LUMINOUS COLLAGE OF POSSIBILITY AND WONDER. RIOTS OF COLOR, POSTERS, POEMS, THRILLING PHOTOGRAPHS, ART PIECES, INVENTIONS, MYSTERIES, PAINTINGS, AND HER MANY BOOKS OF ART AND WORDS.

WHENEVER I VISIT HER, I HAVE TO LIE DOWN IMMEDIATELY AND SOAK IN AS MUCH AS I CAN.

SABRINA IS BOTH ENERGIZING AND RELAXING, AND SHE IS SUCH A LIVING EXAMPLE OF SUCCULENCE.   YES.

ZOE
Arielle

Zoe is just 3,
and I am astounded
by all the love packed
in her tiny body.

Her parents taught her to
stretch her body when she's
crabby, so you'll see her on the
floor, head to knees, repeating
"crabby, stretching, crabby,
stretching."

Zoe is a succulent kid!

Her visible feelings, imagination
festivals, and pure presence are
an ecstasy to know.

She loves nightlife, and is a full
contributing party guest. I thought
I'd lived until I danced with Zoe
(she was naked) to Aretha
Franklin's "respect."

Life with Zoe is A living rAinBOW
And I treAsure Being Her GODMOtHer.
It feels like A Holy trust And A very
Deep Gift. I Also like to tHink Of
Myself As "Auntie MAMe!" GreAt Movie too

These children come to stretch Our
HeArts And fill UP Our souls. Zoe
reminDs Me Of tHe Precious now And to
surrender to life. Precious NOW

WHen I visit Zoe, it DOesn't
MAtter WHAt we DO. we Just Are. we
MiGHt WATCH imAGinAry viDeos, Pet
invisiBle kittens, WHisPer secrets, Or
Just DAnce Ourselves silly.

Zoe is intrinsicAlly lovABle, AnD
connects Me to tHAt little Girl insiDe
Of Myself. Zoe is A HeAler AnD
certAinly My teAcHer in tHe Gifts Of
love.

KiDs
crAWl
THrOUGH

Brigette

Brigette Attended one of my Gatherings, where we uncover creative dreams And choose micromovements to help the process along.

Brigette didn't reveal her real creative dream— which was to have a new job, because she said, "the other people's creative dreams seemed better than mine." So she said she wanted to learn to knit.

After the workshop, I received A letter from Brigette's ex-Boyfriend's mother. She said, "Brigette is A treasure, wasting away in An accounting department. You should hire her."

Brigette travels on stars

We interviewed her for a position at Camp Sark, and saw immediately that she was "the one."

It turned out that she lived a block away! Brigette is psychically one of the most relaxing people I've ever met. She is also very intelligent and insightfull. I admire her quickness and reserve. Brigette has old-soul wisdom and is very youthfully spirited.

She is from Beaver Dam, Wisconsin, which connects us as the "Midwest Girls." Brigette's laugh is high and loud and full of life—she is also very animated and determined.

When I asked her what she watches on television, she replied,

"Do you want to know what I really watch? Letterman, Sesame Street, and the BBC." Somehow, this describes something about her.

Minneapolis Minnesota

Beaver Dam Wisconsin

We love her mom Carol! Hi Carol.

She would also like to be known for her excellent yoga toe stands. Brigette says, "yoga is the key to life."

The word perfectionist might have been invented for Brigette, although I've seen big break-throughs in that area.

Brigette can be picky, dominating, judgmental, and slyly manipulative (it takes one to know one, B!).

She is also full of mischief, joy, and loyalty. I am proud to be her business partner and rely on her wise business sense and intuitive reasoning.

I wish everyone could stand on the solid platform of friendship with Brigette.

Just Don't call her cheesehead.

Succulent Work

We all deserve healthy, succulent work. From a perspective of having had hundreds of jobs, I saw that most work was not.

Work needs humanity and change. Especially corporations.

I believe that the more and better we honor the people who work, the more work will actually be accomplished. Workers need:

Light and Air

nourishing environments

ART: | words | To inspire

Use of color and words to energize and uplift

Flexible schedules to
accommodate families and

Actual personal needs!

Juicy work schedules

Nap rooms! every corporation needs them.

"The more naps you take, the more money
you'll make."

lie down more

This is true and proven and will be
immediately obvious.

More day dreams

Neck and shoulder massage stations.
10 minutes can release hours of frustration
and increase productivity.

Utilize spirit
body
mind

Meditation
stations

exercise and play opportunities!

exercise opportunities
physical movement stretches and releases

WALKING
STRETCHING
YOGA
Gentle GYMS

ADVENTURE TRAVEL too

FEELINGS PROCESS SESSIONS

speak of
resentments
or
stuck places
THAT
Aren't working

TEAMS Can
SHARE CONFLICT
resolution
learn Mediation
skills

Time

SABBATICALS
encourage leaves of ABSENCE
opportunities and structure ACTUAL
"WITH PAY" SABBATICALS AFTER years
of service

MANy COMPANies Are MOViNG
iN THese DirectioNs AND We NeeD
to support AND eNCourAGe others
to DO THE SAME. Help them to see All the Benefits!

    It is CleAr to ME tHAt MANy
PEOPle CreAte At HOME WORK
environments iN ORDer to HAVe
these KINDS OF WORKiNG CONDitioNs.
        We leArN Well By eXAMPle

☆Ask questioNs OF your WORKPlAce
        THe KiNDs of questioNs you need answers to

☆OrGANize tHOuGHtFull presentAtioNs
OF New iDeAs

☆GATHer support iN MANAGEMeNt
        Help MANAGEMENt To Be your Ally

☆BeGiN to CreAte AND WORK iN tHE
KiND OF environments tHAt truly
NOurisH you
        you Will THrive iN tHis NOurisHMENt

if Not, AND iF POSSiBle, Quit WHeN
they're Not!

CAMP SARK

For years, I'd been a starving artist. My work had been ignored, rejected, or misunderstood.

In 1989, I began creating art to sell and communicate with more people. I invented something called spirit cards, which were tiny hand-torn pieces of paper with hand-painted edges and a word in the center.

Y e s

There were 33 cards in a deck, and I handmade about a dozen sets. Then I created a display,

which was a tree branch with spirit cards hanging from the branches.

I also made affirmation books, and released a copy of my poster "How to be an Artist."

All of these things sold very quickly And people WANTED More, so I HANDMADE (THOUSANDS) of CARDS, POSters, And AFFirMAtion BOOKS in A Borrowed GARAGE—I HAD to QUICKly DisAPPeAr wHen the People CAMe HOMe!

The poster CAUGHt the Attention of A PUBlisHer, And I wrote My First BOOK, A CreAtive COMPANion in 1990.

By 1992, I BeCAMe very interested in ForMinG A COMPANy to exPAnD My vision, And so I Hired A Business Mentor to work with Me And HelP Me leArn ABOUt Business. I HAD long Avoided the lineAr world

In 1993/94 I stArted CAMP SARK By renting tHe toP Floor oF A BUilDinG Behind My MAGic CottAGe, Getting A COMPUter, And Hiring An Assistant. Thank you eLizaBeTH! At tHAt point, I wAsn't even sure I could PAy tHe rent For More tHAn A MontH! My Friend LARRy oFFered to Move into it iF I Needed tHAT!

From there, CAMP sARK HAS FlOuriSHeD And exPAnDeD to An ADDitionAl locAtion,

The posters And CARDS TAUGHT Me SUCH Determination

HireD A Design teAM, introDuceD
"SArk's InspireD Gift Collection," AnD
PubliSHeD 2 more BooKs, A MAGIC
Museletter, AnD set UP A web site.
We've BeGun the SARK FounDAtion,
orGAnizeD nAtionAl AnD internAtionAl
Book tours, AnD spoken to Groups
ABout succulence AnD inspirAtion.

   We Are A 3-pArtner COMPAny:
Myself, BriGette, AnD ADrienne. We
Are still GrowinG AnD shApinG our
collective vision.

   I love hAvinG A COMPAny, AnD
sometimes WAnt to AvoiD the Work of
it. Since we process Conflict AnD tell
the truth, there is not MUCH rooM to
HiDe or HolD GruDGes. We Are All
perfectionists, AnD PUSH ourselves,
AnD sometimes eACH other, pretty
HArD.

The DAnces of PerfeCTion CAn Be SUCH A BAlAncinG ACT

We work with a great team of consultants and helpers in Finance, *Thank you Irving*
Thank you Larry & Don   *Thank you Sheila & John*
law, and licensing and are learning all the time about what works in our business and what doesn't. *Thank you Ray!*
   We use volunteer *Thank you* help and publish art and writing of contributors in our Museletters. We've created a five-year plan and are learning how to say (no) as well as (yes) to opportunities. We set our own hours, choose vacations, and try to live and work with the type of company we've always wanted to work for.

Some ingredients of a succulent company:

Proactivity   Truth   Accountability
                     integrity
                     Humor
Humanity   Spirituality   Creativity
                     Community
Trust   Conflict resolution   Conscious
    immediacy   Chocolate   Communication
                     Flowers   inspiration
                     Consistent
                     Love

153

Business Mentoring

I think we are at the beginning of an exciting new time when people in business are choosing to really help and mentor the new businesses being born, especially in the realms of creative conscious businesses. This is being written of and explored within the context of a newly defined group called the "cultural creatives." These people are revisiting and questioning their careers, their personal pursuits and quality of their lives, weaving together an integration and balance of all these elements. There is much more to "cultural creatives" than business

I was mentored in my business by a man named Ray Davi. I worked with him as I set up my new business, and called it "Business Olympics" because, for a free-spirited, nonlinear person like me, it was a challenge to stay focused and

Business Olympics

complete tasks. Thanks to Ray and the work, I discovered that I had many talents in business and could begin to act powerfully in that realm.

I learned about professional communications, proactive planning, meeting protocol and presentations, business accountability, and envisioning the future for my company, while living squarely in the present.

During my year with Ray, my business doubled in income and found a secure place from which to operate. Ray was the first to ask me, "What about your personal life? When do you have time for it?"

WHAT ABOUT MY PERSONAL LIFE?

After 14 years of being self-employed, I'D worked 7 days a week for so long that weekends were unknown to me. There certainly wasn't space or time for a love life...

He helped me see the necessity of separating myself from the business and letting it grow as an individual entity. This was a difficult concept for me to grasp, and Ray challenged me by asking if I could get my ego out of it. I'm still working on this!

We all have so much to offer each other in business. You can adopt and be adopted by other businesses to accelerate growth and explore new paths in business.

Because we can truly all learn and grow together

If you are working within a company and want to be part of a change process, see if you can adopt someone from the organization who will support you and your unique contributions. Or, form a group with other workers to implement suggestions for growth and change. However large or small a business or corporation is, it is still a group of people, one by one, that makes it come alive.

Our connections are more than we know

ray davi · personal & professional mentor
raymond davi creative management
Carmel, California

Being A Mentor

Use interns and volunteers in a conscious way to share your business ways with other people.

Submit and contribute interviews and articles being written on this subject.

Run your company as an open book— share information willingly and seek opportunities to assist others.

Write your mission statement and share it.

Needing A Mentor

Study companies that you like and admire.

Seek volunteer or intern possibilities.

Ask about mentoring programs and/or if you can help start one.

Find kindred spirits in business and request their assistance.

Readings:

Visionary Business
            By Marc Allen

Six Months Off
        By Hope Dlugozima
        James Scott
        David Sharp

SARK FOUNDATION

As our company, CAMP SARK, continues to grow, we will keep finding new ways to help others grow.

Here is our mission statement:

CAMP SARK is a company that designs and creates products for creative living. Our mission is to spread the spirit of SARK—a philosophy that says we are each creatively gifted and need to share those gifts. Our goals are to touch many lives through various projects, products, and philanthropy, to provide inspirational nourishment, encourage people to listen to their creative souls, and in turn, help to transform the world.

Our vision For the SARK
Foundation includes linking with
like-minded companies to help us
Form And Find programs that will:

* Get Art BACK into the
schools we need All the creativity tools for our kids!
* Help libraries Be prosperous rich libraries
* inspire And protect children
the children need us

We Are Formulating plans For
women's causes And
environmental concerns And will
continue to Dedicate A portion of
profits From our company For
those purposes.

Marvelous
purposes

We can all begin in tiny, medium, or large ways, to invent and execute creative solutions for our many challenges.

Whenever I see ads for moving or maintenance, they often say,

(no job too small!)

none of our efforts are too small.

we are not small

We can become paralyzed by the enormity of problems, yet the human spirit is larger than any of these.

everything
is just waiting
to be made up by us!

MAGiC COTTAGE

One of the most succulent spots I know of is my home, which I call the Magic Cottage.

It used to be a toolshed and is only 180 square feet in size. There is no real furniture except for a loft bed, a hanging chair, and some big pillows.

One wall is all windows and there are beams on the ceiling and a wooden floor.

Outside the front door is a garden 3 times the size of the cottage.

The glorious overgrown garden

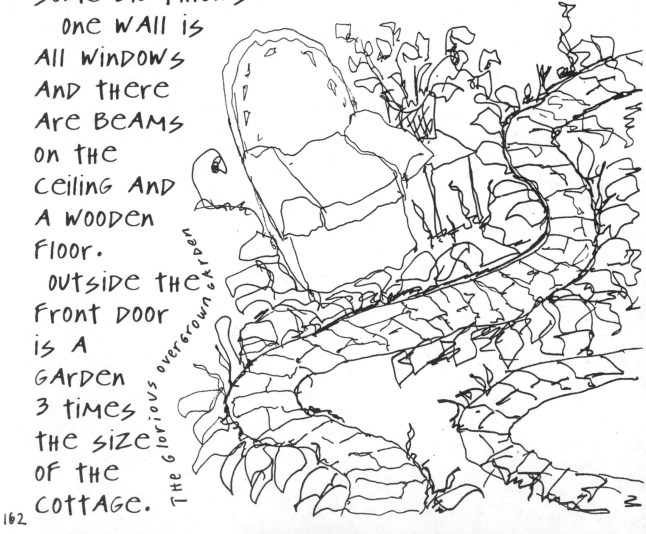

THis GArden is extremely overGrown And filled with layers of leAves And WHAt I CAll My "science experiments," WHICH Are crumbling pieces of entropy that I enjoy WATCHinG, SUCH As BrACkish WAter in A vAse-just WHAt will Grow in there if left Alone long enouGH? or A CHAir entwined with vines-WHAt reAlly Holds it toGether?

RAMPANT IVY

A WAyWArd PlAnt HAs Grown From the GArden Through the WAll into the cottAGe. It's the size of A smAll tree And fills most of one corner.

I CAll it My "Free plAnt" it MAkes My Friend BriGette nervous

My friend Larry calls the Magic Cottage "Wild Kingdom" because of all the creatures and nature that reside here. Racoons, hawks, baby foxes, slugs, snails, butterflies, spiders, birds, mosquitoes, lizards, and a flock of very loud wild parrots.

The wild parrots fly low and clumsy. We call them "the thugs"

It is a very special spot in the midst of the big city of San Francisco.

I go outside at night in my pajamas and sit listening to the trees, while my black cat Jupiter hunts moths.

sometimes he just watches

I write all of my books lying
down on a futon beneath the loft
bed, surrounded by books, cards,
quotes, divinations, affirmations,
magnifying glasses, bits of dyed
string, special shells, sparkling
rocks, photos, and cigar boxes
full of fascinations.

   There are
shelves of
old journals
and here is
what I wrote in
one of them about the cottage
when I first moved in:

MY
MAGnificent
Life

82 87 85 86 86 86

   The chimes have come fully
alive here, their sounds follow me
everywhere.

Woodsmoke escorts me down the cobbled path strewn with crackled leaves and bits of colored flower petals.

The wind catches my rainbow banner and spanks it, reminding me of Bahamian sailing adventures.

Beyond the pale blue fence, I can feel the ocean.

The cobbled path

One candle lights my atmosphere, and illuminates the wooden beams on the ceiling and leads me to wonder who has loved here before me?

One candle lights my atmosphere

I used to be afraid of spiders...

There are creatures here, slugs in the bathroom, spiders spinning in corners.

166

A secretive mouse somewhere near the kitchen, a giant moth lying flat on the windowshade.

There is a silence here, a polished gleaming quiet punctuated by foghorns from the sea.   s i l e n c e

The shower causes me to laugh as I stand on wood slats near the toilet and aim the massage spray all over my body. A sexual healing has taken place here, a reclaiming of some immensely private part of myself, lost long ago.

Rocks and shells and pieces of bark belong here. It is a ship, a Paris garret, an island hideaway, a fantasy treehouse.

I am warm and safe and happy here. I am home at last.

AUStrALiA

THe First thing tHAt stArtled Me there WAs tHe Money: it is Brightly colored, slippery, With cleAr HoloGrAMs in the corners BordereD With tiny stArs. There Are WoMEN's FACes on tHeir Money!

I WAs in AustrAliA For A Book tour With <u>Succulent</u> <u>WiLD</u> <u>Woman</u> AnD My Business pArtner Brigette AnD I were scooped into Adventures All AlonG the WAy.

We cuddled with KoAlAs, WAndered in A Field oF prehistoric-lookinG KAnGAroos, Were invited to Be in the cockpit oF A Jet DurinG lAnDinG, sAW the Green FlAsh At sunset over the IndiAn oceAn, AnD AttendeD ABoriGinAl AWAKeninG ceremonies.

We met with the Artist Ken Done, Ken Done is rare
who is a painter of great electricity
and spirit. We fell in love with 2
singers called "the Velvet Janes." Mardi & Rose These women Are Awesomely Gifted

It is very good for a worrier to
be in a country that says "no
worries!" to everything. "No worries!"

The people are eccentric and
outspoken. A room service waiter
commented on the flowers in my
hotel room, "My, your tulips have
opened just magnificently!"

A man getting into an elevator
called me a "big loner" when I
admitted that I'd rather ride down
by myself. We experienced such
generosity, hospitality, and open
hearts from most of the BIG
Australians we met. OPEN HEARTS

I appeared on the show "Good
Morning Australia," and when I told
the host that I thought the

Australians were eccentric, he responded by throwing his legs on top of the coffee table on his set and grinning.

There is such a great succulent energy in Australia. It is large and humming with adventure.

☆ The stars are different there!

I want to go back and run through red dirt, stay in a rain forest, swim at the Great Barrier reef, make love beneath the southern cross in the sky. Australia filled me with wonder and opened up my idea of the world. Now I want to travel through Africa and Bali.

One very curious thing about Australia: the electricity there caused the top of my vibrator to blow off and shoot across the room.

Yes, I had an adaptor.

I did _not_ adapt well to this turn of events.

Big Sur

The Air is juicy Here. The land is wild. I think there is A vortex that keeps certain people From coming to Big Sur.

I've Been exploring Big Sur For 15 years, And Have Barely touched its essence. There Are secrets in its Canyons And Among the people.

There is something uncontained in those that live here— it challenges the soul And spirit.

The Beauty in Big Sur is ragged And Proud. It is stern in nature's way—weather, wild Animals, And the one road cut into the rocks, which is closed off After certain Fierce storms.

STEEP DROP OFF

I AM Drawn to the Deep Fog, Giant Blackbirds, And Brilliant ocean sunsets.

Big Sur MAgnifies Discontents, And can Deepen sadnesses. I Don't think I could live there, And I somehow like knowing this.

I marvel at the star-crowded sky and the big, breathing redwood trees.

There are such serendipitous spots here: The Henry Miller Library, Esalen, Deetjens, Ventana, Pfeiffer Beach... Visit Henry Miller Library. Yum.

I am awed by the magnificent gifts of nature in all her succulence.

I've experienced so many gorgeous and unusual moments in Big Sur. One night at twilight, I was walking down from watching a sunset and a big bird of some kind flapped overhead. The darkness deepened very quickly and I hadn't brought a flashlight and could barely see the rutted path. I suddenly felt very frightened and stopped for a moment. I then heard the loud squawk of this bird, and realized it had landed somewhere in front of me. This bird escorted me all the way down the mountain, stopping every 5 feet or so to wait for me to catch up. The squawking began to sound like laughter, and the bird and I made it safely back to lamplight together.

The solace of lamplight

172

Living More Succulently
Being A Student of Succulence

Nature is already succulent. I believe we must be the students of that succulence. While walking on a beach in Carmel at sunset, my friend Ray and I saw a spiral drawn in the sand. Ray exclaimed at the succulent shape, and we walked towards it.

At that moment, another friend of ours, Tori, emerged from behind some rocks and we all hugged. We joked about her having lured us with this succulent shape—we then ran around the spiral together, and joined exuberantly in the center of it.

Later, I found out that Tori had not even drawn the spiral, and had happened upon it just like we had!

We are often called to succulence by serendipity and synchronicity.

If we place ourselves squarely in the swirl of life, it will scoop us up and change us somehow. The trick is to come out of hiding, change our routines, and allow our actual lives to happen.

The sunset walk I had taken wasn't particularly convenient, and didn't fit into the evening's schedule, yet I knew I had to be in that beach twilight. How many beach sunsets will we see?

We Must

We must walk outside in white socks, tie yellow ribbons on all the lampposts, The cheerful rocks collect cheerful rocks, and watch children dance by firelight. Let's see more shooting stars, look deep into cows' eyes, and walk barefoot outside. Let's take sudden drives north to somewhere new,

174

Write A BOOK ABOut our lovers, AnD BAKe cookies in the shapes of AnimAls.

Let's weAr PAJAMAs to church, tAKe squAre DAnce lessons, AnD refuse to Do Dishes For A weeK.

our succulence AWAits us. We Are MADe for succulence-our succulent heArtBeAts will leAD the wAy.

Follow your succulence! It coulD leAD you to PicK hunDreDs of tiny DAisies, or As My FrienDs SABrinA AnD NiKKi DiD, GAther wilDFlowers in BunChes AnD weAr them As "BreAst Bouquets." FinD A stAtue AnD write it A love note, Borrow A DOG AnD GO on A Picnic toGether, CliMB A crooKeD tree AnD sit in the BrAnches reADinG.

FinD someone WHo needs HeLP anD Give it

CrooKeD BrAnches MAKe GreAt SeAts

175

Issue A statement of succulence

I _____ AM
succulent
This is A natural, True, and good Thing.

Take your succulence into the world with you And:
refuse to live A narrow, Airless life!
Stand up on A plane And read poetry (out loud). Bestow compliments to other passengers in the elevator. Send notes of Admiration (Anonymously).

Make A move in **any** new direction.

You Are remarkable

Let the world speak succulently to you.

One time, I was in New York in deep summer, And I'd gone Alone to A free concert in Central Park.

It WAS very crowDeD, and still I Felt incredibly lonely. I WALKeD AWAY, intending to Go BACK to My Hotel, WHen I sank to the GRASS and Asked For A succulent sign.

I looKeD up to see HunDreds of twinKLing Lights Darting through the Humid Air. They were All Around Me in A Glittering cloud.
FireFlies!
The MiRACle of the FireFlies HeAled Me that niGHT.

the FireFlies DanceD in the niGHT sKY

" THe Breeze AT DAWn HAS secrets to tell you.
    Don't Go BACK to sleep.
You MUST ASK For WHAT you really want.
    Don't Go BACK to sleep.
People Are GoinG BACK and Forth Across the Doorsill
    WHere the two worLDs touch.
The Door is round and open.
    Don't Go BACK to sleep."
                        RUMi

177

we Are succulent!

We Are succulent with our shredded fantasies, our unread books, our misguided perfectionism, our hiding in bed eating rows of cookies, or neurotically running to and away from things.

We Are succulent JUST LIKE THIS. JUST the way we are NOW.

Our mysteries, our insanities, our relentless self-improvement programs Are All pieces of succulence.

We Are succulent HALF finished, in process, eyes swollen from crying and denying our weaknesses.

We Are this.

We Are succulent.

How ODD. It can feel like there is so much to DO.

THe tending of All of our pArts 🌙 ✧
Becomes Full time, seeming to block out
Spontaneous moondances and playing Bingo
NAKeD.

We MUST continue to...

it softens All our
edges

celeBRAte THe moon

We lie in our BeDs,
Hoping For enouGH sleep to repeAT the DO·DO
of yesterDAy. We Are propelled From our BeDs, into A
B U S Y Life.

Yet the reAL succulence occurs in the
GAPs, the in·Be tweens, the unexpected moments
of luxury in our SOULs.

It is the unplanned life, the Being truLy
Alive in eACH moment.
(WHATever) thAT moment might contain.

All thAT We DO NOt DO is succulent Also.

JUST TO Be A HUMan Bean
is the ULtiMAte BODACious SUCCulent AcT !

179

Succulence

TO ORDER
SARK's First 5 books:
A Creative companion,
Inspiration Sandwich, SARK's
Journal & play! book, Living Juicy,
The Magic cottage Address book

Ask your favorite bookstore!

or call: Celestial Arts
1·800·841·BOOK
(2665)

or write: P.O. Box 7327
Berkeley, CA 94707

A portion of the royalties from this book will be donated to charitable organizations

For SARK's MAGIC MUSELETTER
Please see the last page of this book for an invitation to this succulent subscription!

To order Audiotapes of
A Creative companion and Succulent
Wild Woman please call: Audio
Literature at 1·800·383·0174

CALL 1·415·546·EPIC
(3742)
For the inspiration Line
BY SARK
3-5 minute recorded message
BY SARK 24 hours a day
A great place to give and receive inspiration!

connects us ALL

TO REACH US AT CAMP SARK :
(you'll be included   PO BOX 330039
on SARK's   SARKFrancisco CA 94133
MAGIC MAILING
LIST)

e-MAIL: CAMPSARK@BEST.COM

PLEASE visit us on the WEB! WWW.CAMPSARK.COM

For General information and A peek into
SARK's creative schedule, CALL
            415. 397. SARK
               (7275) 24 HrS. A DAY

LOOK For SARK's inspired Gift
collection! in stores near you
(CARDS, notecards, posters, prints, Blankets, & More!)
For More information on How To purchase
SARK Gift items, CALL portal Publications AT
800. 255. 1849 For A recorded Message.

TO order SUCCULENT WILD WOMAN or More copies of
the BODACIOUS BOOK of SUCCULENCE (and other Simon &
Schuster titles) CALL: 1. 800. 223. 2336
            Fax: 1. 800. 445. 6991
or write: SIMON & SCHUSTER 200 OLD TAppan road
                        OLD TAppan, new Jersey 07675
Visit SIMON SAYS web site: HTTP://www. simonSAys.com For A LIST
of All Simon & SCHUSTER Titles - LOOK For SARK!
CALL Special Sales with regards to special Discounts For either title
For Groups or teachers: 212. 654. 8552

To THE AMAZING AUSTRALIA

BIG. reALLY BIG. HUGE.

Always, to the wild parrots

THE BiG THANK YOU!

WE ARE ALL DEEPLY CONNECTED- even MORE THAN WE KNOW.

I THANK eACH one of you DEAR SOULS reADing THiS. I SeND you MY Love.

TO KOALAS

TO Susan Brett Again, TransformaTion?

With Love to SARAH, for college and Beyond

TO PAM WALLACE : Madeleine DiAngelo spiritual writers/warriors

TO erica Carlisle NAKeD PASSiON DANCiNG

TO Joe Brown of San Francisco AND Beyond

To anne lamoTT For words oF TruTH

In celebration of cake!

To JULiA CAMeron

A very special Thank you to Gary Rosenthal my Guide in TruTh AND consciousness AND remarkable poet.

♡To my niece emily claire

TO MY MONDAY Night Group: rADiANT essence workers

TO the FABuLous steele FAMiLy: Sherpa, zoe, Ken, ADriENNE THiS FAMiLy DeFiNes Love

To Dan PauL i liviNG The MYSTERY Mystery

To Arlene BernsTein succulent fruits and vegetables

2 AbsoluTely DeAr souls

TO MAyA ANGeLou For enveloping Soul essence

TO CHeri HuBer succulent SweAT

With love of FAMily & HilDegard

TO BoB Bressy eccentric words & wisdom

TO PAT D And in MArvelous MEMORY of Luvy

Cecilia/steve Lulu Love

ELizabeth Kayser writer/ rocker/ jokey/heARTS/ Deep heART

TO Perth AND THE INDIAN OCEAN

With love roDY/Posin ALLowing Spirit

special THANKS to Irving Bernstein Accounting For ANGels

KATheriNe russell Novelist

TO elEANor rare LigHT

TO Brigette-KoALA Hugger endearing Friend, Honest Business PARTNER and Midwest companion

To LouiS♡ needs A MASSAGE AND will love it! With love to ANNeD KeL Geddes Thanks for creative support!

To PM WALLACE:

TO Angela♡LArry JustiN, JoRDAN FAMiLy of KiNDNess

TO SABRINA A HuMAN ANGeL & Deep Friend to me

TO SUSAN B encampmenTS of The SOuL

TO eLiSSA A very DeAr Friend of Mine, and of essence

TO CATHY and KAThLEEN 2 angels to my MoM

TO Valerie♡Seattle With love

TO MY MOM (AND Toby) AKA "MArvelous MARjorie" AKA "ADorable ToO"

To robin♡JoAN A TeAM of love AND HuMor

TO NicoLe young MY TrAPEZe MATe

TO SusAn♡Michael Gracious souls

To andrew HistoriAN & HuMAN and conflict

TO McNAiR WiTH ALL MY Love DEEPLy We GO TOGETHER iT ALL WiTH Love

see dog

WiTH love to JupiTer

TO Larry Allen rosenthal PH.D (peace, Harmony, Desire) WiTH Love

TO R.A.Y. DAVi AMBASSADOR To SARK and rADiant Active yes

With love to ViMALA: A,D,G,Q,V,Y,W.

TO HAR BOR IsLAND TO HOMEOPATHY TO

TO THe SARK angels: KeMBY, noelle, SARAH, LorA Bless each one of you!

TO VANessA BLOOMiNG GODDESS with love ATTiTuDE

TO iSABEL Collins WiTH DEEP Love

TO ADrienne DeArest Friend, Trusted Business PartNer and MotHer of Zoe!

TO DiANA ♡ George My Deluxe FAiRy GoDPARents

TO Tori A MenTor of Wellness

TO Debbie edwards youDANCiNG HEART

JOHN♡LOiS Gifted intuitives

TO Katie Grant Awe-inspiring Actor of love and LiFe!

With love to STeLLA 2nd PilATes→new breATh

TO SAM keen and His Trapeze ranch

TO rich BLAKE FooT Hero

TO andrea scher vaLUABLe MEMBer of CAMP SARK and Gifted ARTiST

Here's to JASON HeiDeMANN VALUABLE CAMP SARK MEMBer and DeAr SOuL

TO THe rug BARN: KeNDAL ADAMS and Kitty Thomson · WHAT WiLD, wonDerFuL Folks!

TO POrTAL PuBLicATIONS: For SHAriNG Our viSiON THANK you

To My PEN neigHBorS: SALLy, MicHAeL, Curtis & nancy, speeDy!, ricHARD, JohNATHAN

TO ALL THe MeDiA escorts AND BOOKstores on THe succulent wild woman Book tour!

With love to MARDi· ROSE· ZAC

TO JenNifer and THe GoDDESSES AT THe inspiration FActory Blessings

TO Cynthia For FOOD of the Goddesses

TO SAM,the airline angel

MArcie · Den HeArT

HeLeN SANDers

cARO, ernie!

To PiNk SANDS

Bless you All AT CHez Panisse!

TO everyone AT WiLLiam Morris I still think THe percenTages Are FAir.

TO DeBRA GoLDStein A remarkable AND visionAry AGenT, wise Friend AND Trusted Traveling companion.

TO Ken DoNe who helped me MAKe iT ALL reAL Bless you.

TO ALL AT SiMoN & SCHUSTer

TO MAry ann NAPLeS A reALLy SMART eDiTor, Gifted writer AND plAiN-SPEAKiNG Friend.

SPeCiAL THANks to CArlene BAver wHO KNows MY LAUGH...

With Help These Books stay eccentric

MArcie · Den HeArT AND speciAL THAnks TO THe wHole TeAM AUsTrALiA-To RANDOM House

SARK'S MAGIC Museletter

You * Are A Gift

There is A MAGIC cottage inside each of us

DEAR ANGEL FACES,

[Left handwritten letter - partially legible]

I AM ALWAYS WANTING HEALING TO OCCUR IN A STRAIGHT LINE, OR IN SOME KIND OF "CONNECT THE DOTS" MAP. SOME PART OF ME IS ALWAYS COUNTING-THE NUMBER OF MONTHS SINCE MY FATHER'S DEATH, THE NUMBER OF YEARS SINCE I SPOKE WITH MY OLDER BROTHER. IT ISN'T HEALING TOOK PLACE IN SOME KIND OF REASONABLE PATTERN!

THE SEDUCTION OF A PATTERN IS SO THAT I CAN PREDICT, FORESEE, OR CONTROL THE OUTCOME. I THINK "AFTER MORE THAN A YEAR SINCE MY FATHER'S DEATH, I SHOULD BE FEELING _____."

I BELIEVE THAT HEALING HAPPEN IN SPURTS AND LAYERS AND INSIDE INTERIOR CREVICES. IT COMES AT 4 AM WHILE WATCHING THE MOON, OR UNEXPECTEDLY SOBBING AT A BOOKSTORE WHEN YOU SPOT A PARTICULAR BOOK THAT YOU WOULD HAVE BOUGHT FOR YOUR FATHER. AND THEN YOU STOP AND SUDDENLY REMEMBER THAT HE IS DEAD.

WHILE ON VACATION THIS MONTH, I EXPERIENCED A HEALING REALIZATION WHILE WALKING ON A SANDY PATH BY FROM THE BEACH. DURING MY CAMP CALENDAR, MY FATHER TRAVELED CATCHINESS ON BUSINESS AND WAS GONE MOST OF EACH WEEK. I HAVE KNOWN FOR A LONG TIME ABOUT THE LOSS AND ABANDONMENT I EXPERIENCED, BUT THIS WAS AN INTELLECTUAL KNOWING. I WAS VACATIONING WITH MY DEAR FRIEND ADRIENNE, WHO WAS SPENDING FIVE DAYS AWAY FROM HER TWO YEAR-OLD DAUGHTER ZOE. I WEEPED ABOUT HOW MUCH SHE MISSED HER MOM, AND REALIZED THAT MY DAD LIKE THIS EVERY WEEK. SOME PART OF ME MADE HIM NOT REAL SO THAT IT WOULDN'T HURT SO MUCH. I SEE MYSELF REVERSE THIS DYNAMIC NOW WITH THE MEN I LOVE. WHEN WE'RE APART FOR A CERTAIN AMOUNT OF TIME, I BEGIN DISMANTLING THE RELATIONSHIP IN SOME WAYS, AND DISTANCE MYSELF, AND MAKE HIM NOT REAL SO THAT I DON'T EXPERIENCE LOSS.

I FELL TO MY KNEES ON THAT SANDY BEACH PATH, AND CRIED THE HOT TEARS OF A YOUNG CHILD.

HEALING DOESN'T CARE ABOUT THE YEARS. I THINK IT IS AGELESS AND TIMELESS. IT WAITS FOR OUR SOULS TO LEAP INTO ACCEPTANCE.

I BELIEVE WE CAN HEAL OURSELVES, AND IN SO DOING, BECOME "STRONGER AT THE BROKEN PLACES" (FROM WAYNE MULLER'S BOOK, "LEGACY OF THE HEART").

I HAVE SO MANY BROKEN PLACES AND INTEND TO STAY CLOSE TO THE HEALING SPIRALS AND MYSTERIES OF THE SOUL.

I WISH FOR YOU:

THE WILLINGNESS TO LOOK RIGHT AT THE SADDEST PARTS OF YOURSELF, AND ALLOW HEALING TO TAKE PLACE

TO THINK OF YOURSELF AS "COMMITTED TO HEALING" IN YOUR LIFE AND OTHERS' LIVES.

TO EXPLORE HEALING IN NEW, UNFAMILIAR WAYS

I SEND TO YOU:

A CLEAR LIGHT SHINING INSIDE OF YOU THAT HEALS SPOTS.

A SUMMER ADVENTURE OUTDOORS, NAKED IN WATER

A MOONLIGHT PICNIC

A DEEP HUMMING SOUND FROM WAY INSIDE YOU THAT VIBRATES YOUR BONES

THE ARTICULATION OF PAIN AND THE ALLOWING OF YOUR HEALING IMAGINATION

SPONTANEOUS PRAYERS

TO SPEND HALF TIME WITH A CHILD

TO SIT IN YOUR OWN ESSENCE, HOLDING THE TINY CHILD INSIDE YOURSELF IN A HEALING VISION

AND A NO HANDS BIKE RIDE!

For Love And Healing,
SARK

[caption] ACTUAL SIZE 17x24 INCHES

DEAR ANGEL FACES,

Welcome to your personal invitation to the MAGIC Museletter! There is a large plant growing through the wall of my Magic Cottage here in San Francisco. This Museletter reminds me of a magnificent, magical plant that sprouted from a dream, and is now growing into the homes of all my readers.

The Museletter was born in 1996 and now goes out to thousands of amazing people. It is the result of a wonder-full collaboration between my business partners and the entire CAMP SARK clan to produce and write this for you and also features your writing, support, and feedback.

A subscription to the MAGIC Museletter enables us to mail to you huge, full-color, consistent, exciting pieces of art on a regular basis. This is so exciting to me! I myself read and get inspired by the Museletter all the time! It includes snippets of conversation, wild imaginings, and peeks into cottage life with me. I write a letter for you in each issue and I look forward to talking with you and having you along for the fun and adventure of it all!

I send you a dream cape, a hat that keeps out negativity, and goblets of inspiration.

Very Dearly, SARK

Here's WHAT YOU CAN look forward to in the Museletter:

- Each issue includes a 17" x 24" Inspirational letter from SARK that focuses on different themes. Some back issue themes have included: Healing, Friendship, Succulence, and Comfort

- SARK's Purple Backpack Adventures–A Traveler's Guide to Serendipity

- Inner Views–Wild Imaginings with highly creative people (which we all are!)

- Subscriber's Contribute–An opportunity for your art and writing to be published in the Museletter!

- SARK's latest calendar & book gathering dates.

- Ripe News from Camp and more!

To order back issues of the Museletter send check or money orders for $4.50 (includes shipping and handling-$6.50 for all foreign orders, in U.S. funds only please!) to Camp SARK, Attn: ML Back issues, PO Box 330039, SF, CA 94133.

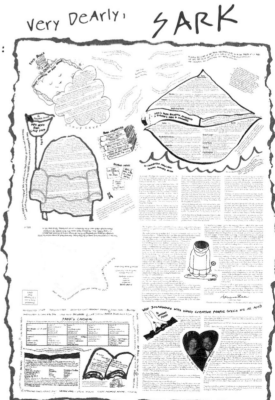

[caption] ACTUAL SIZE 17x24 INCHES

 Yes!

Please sign me up to receive a two-year, eight-issue subscription of **SARK's Magic Museletter.**

Please send this card (see below) and payment to:

Camp SARK
Attn: Museletter, PO Box 330039,
San Francisco, CA 94133

Rates are as follows: Regular–$23, "**Star** achie**ving** Artist"–$19.50, Child 12 & Under–$19.50, All Foreign Orders–$28 *(payable in U.S. funds only) Checks or money orders accepted. Checks made payable to Camp SARK.*

 Send a Friend a Gift! *to my succulent friend...*

There will be so much inspiration and information in **SARK's Magic Museletter,** you'll want to share it with your friends and family. The Museletter is a unique gift to give and to receive. It will provide two years' worth of creativity and fun at a great price! Please choose a rate for your gift subscription and send it along with your payment to the above address. A gift card will be sent to the recipient to announce their new subscription.

Please allow 6-8 weeks for delivery of your first issue.

SARK'S Magic Museletter
Subscriber Information
(Please print clearly!)

1

Name	Phone #	E-mail

Address	City	State	Zip (+4 digits)

Rates: *(circle one)*   Regular–$23   "Starving Artist"–$19.50   Child 12 & Under–$19.50
All Foreign Orders–$28 *(payable in U.S. funds only)*

2

Name	Phone #	E-mail

Address	City	State	Zip (+4 digits)

Rates: *(circle one)*   Regular–$23   "Starving Artist"–$19.50   Child 12 & Under–$19.50
All Foreign Orders–$28 *(payable in U.S. funds only)*

Order 1 is a Gift Subscription* from: _____

Order 2 is a Gift Subscription* from: _____

Checks or money orders accepted. Checks made payable to Camp SARK.
Please allow 6-8 weeks for delivery of your first issue.
*A gift card will be mailed to recipient.